INJECTING INCENTIVES INTO THE ACHIEVEMENT OF SOCIAL AND ENVIRONMENTAL OUTCOMES: SOCIAL POLICY BONDS

Injecting Incentives Into the Achievement of Social and Environmental Outcomes: Social Policy Bonds

Ronnie Horesh

Writers Club Press

San Jose New York Lincoln Shanghai

Injecting Incentives Into the Achievement of Social and Environmental Outcomes: Social Policy Bonds

Writers Club Press
an imprint of iUniverse, Inc.

For information address:
iUniverse, Inc.
5220 S. 16th St., Suite 200
Lincoln, NE 68512
www.iuniverse.com

ISBN: 0-595-24823-3

Printed in the United States of America

Contents

Introduction

This book describes a new financial instrument, Social Policy Bonds, whose purpose is to make government spending more focused and cost-effective. 'Government spending' means here the costs of interventions by all levels of government—local, national, and supranational—to its citizens.

The first chapter briefly tries to show that government spending in the developed countries is significant and that much of it is misdirected, wasteful or even counterproductive. Chapter 2 outlines in brief how Social Policy Bonds could inject market incentives into the solution of social and environmental problems. Chapter 3 looks at some of the practical aspects and potential pitfalls of a Social Policy Bond regime, and at how a transition to such a regime could best be managed. Chapter 4 looks at the likely advantages of Social Policy Bonds compared with the current policymaking system. Chapter 5 compares Social Policy Bonds with other 'more market' approaches to policy, while Chapter 6 looks in more detail at the political aspects of using the bonds in developed and developing countries. The seventh and final chapter assesses looks at the objectives that governments might target with Social Policy Bonds, and at implications of a bond regime for politics in the future. A brief epilogue concludes the book.

There are two detailed examples of Social Policy Bond issues: the first, targeting climate change, in chapter 4; the second, targeting illiteracy in developing countries, in chapter 6.

1

Government spending in the developed countries

There are two main reasons for believing that it is important to get value for taxpayers' money. The first is that the sums involved are large; the second that people are compelled to pay tax and that such an infringement of freedom ought not to be taken lightly. This chapter begins by looking at government spending in the developed countries, and then goes on to consider its efficiency.

GOVERNMENT SPENDING

Just how important is government spending? For current purposes, a useful measure is government spending as a proportion of Gross Domestic Product (GDP). For the developed countries the current average is around 36.5 per cent. There are variations, but as table 1 shows, the broad trend was for this proportion to rise until the mid 1990s, despite efforts in some countries to make cutbacks and 'roll back the frontiers of the state'. The main source of upward pressure on spending over this period in nearly all countries was the establishment and expansion of programmes in the social policy domain (public pensions, income support, health care, education and other public services).[1]

Note that these are proportions of a GDP that has been rising. Together these facts mean that despite the recent dip in proportionate

outlays over the past few years, government spending continues to
grow in absolute terms.

Table 1. General government outlays, by country, per cent of GDP [*]

	1965	1975	1985	1990	1995	2000[**]
Australia	24.6	31.3	37.8	33.0	35.4	31.4
Austria	36.6	44.4	50.1	48.5	52.4	48.8
Belgium	35.0	47.6	57.3	50.8	50.3	46.7
Canada	27.8	38.9	45.4	46.0	45.3	37.8
Denmark [***]	31.8	47.1	58.0	53.6	56.6	51.3
Finland	30.3	37.0	42.3	44.4	54.3	44.8
France	37.6	42.3	51.9	49.6	53.6	51.2
Germany	35.3	47.1	45.6	43.8	46.3	43.0
Greece	22.0	27.1	42.3	47.8	46.6	43.7
Ireland	36.0	40.7	50.5	39.5	37.6	27.7
Italy	32.8	41.0	50.6	53.1	52.3	46.7
Japan	19.0	26.8	31.6	31.3	35.6	38.2
Korea	14.5	16.9	17.6	18.3	19.3	23.4
Mexico	..	..	..	..	21.4	..
Netherlands	34.7	45.7	51.9	49.4	47.7	41.5
Norway	29.1	39.8	41.5	49.7	47.6	40.6
Portugal***	18.1	25.2	42.9	44.2	41.2	42.1
Spain	19.5	24.1	39.4	41.4	44.0	38.5
Sweden	33.5	47.3	59.9	55.8	62.1	53.9
UK***	33.5	44.4	44.0	41.9	44.4	38.4
US	25.6	32.3	33.8	33.6	32.9	29.3
OECD	26.9	34.4	38.1	38.0	39.4	36.5

*   *Sources:* OECD *Economic Outlook* 68, December 2000, OECD National
     Accounts and OECD calculations.
**   Estimates
*** Before 1988 for Denmark, 1995 for Portugal and 1987 for UK, data are
     backward extrapolations based on earlier National Accounts series.

On what are these outlays spent? There are four broad government
expenditure categories:

- Transfers and subsidies (13.6 per cent of GDP, in the year 2000, for
  the countries in table 1). This expenditure category includes income
  support, unemployment benefits, invalidity and single parent benefits, and old age pensions.

- Public consumption (15.7 per cent): services such as defence, law
  and order, education, housing and health;

- Interest on national debt (3.8 per cent): government borrowing to
  pay for all its other activities.

- Public investment (3.4 per cent).

Government's share of Gross Domestic Product is not an infallible
measure of the role of government in the economy, but it is useful as a
rough and ready indicator. Note that, in addition to the taxes necessary
for its budgetary outlays, government intervenes in other ways that
impose additional costs on society. A prime example would be trade
barriers, which keep the prices of imports high.

Government spending merits scrutiny simply by virtue of its size. If
government were inefficient that would affect all its citizens, but it
would be the poorest members of society who suffer most from badly
designed government programmes.

IS GOVERNMENT EFFICIENT?

Perhaps the most flagrant evidence that much government expenditure is misdirected comes in the form of perverse subsidies. These can be defined as subsidies that are economically inefficient *and* socially inequitable *and* environmentally destructive. Most agricultural subsidies fall into this category. Support to producers in the developed countries as measured by the Organisation for Economic Cooperation and Development (OECD) amounted to $311 billion in the year 2001.[2] Most assistance continues to be given in the form of market price support and output payments. These forms of support insulate farmers from world markets and impose a burden on domestic consumers. They also badly distort production and trade, harming especially farmers in developing countries, and intensifying pressure on the environment. As well, being strongly correlated with output levels, they go mostly to the largest farmers. In the US, for instance, about 88 per cent of support goes to the largest (in terms of gross sales) 25 per cent of the farmers. And the higher food prices that result from these policies bear most heavily on low-income consumers, for whom food constitutes a larger share of total household expenditure. Apart from large farmers, many of whom are very wealthy by any standards, the main beneficiaries of the panoply of agricultural support policies in the developed countries are the agribusiness industry and programme administrators,[3] while fraudsters also gain substantially.[4]

    Others benefiting from lavish perverse subsidies in the rich countries are the road transport and energy sectors. Subsidies to private road transport include the hidden costs of providing road users with roads, space and complementary traffic services such as highway patrols, traffic management, and paramedics. For the years 1991 and 1989, two different studies estimated the net subsidies to road transport in the US at $55 billion and $174 billion, respectively, or 1 and 3 per cent respectively of that country's GDP.[5] (The wide range reflects the different estimates for parking subsidies and for providing complementary traffic services.) Questionable on many grounds road funding—as well as funding for public transport schemes—would appear to be another example of middle-class welfare. Most of the benefits of these works go overwhelmingly to those who have more money to spend on travel, and more time in which to do so.[6]

In the mid 1990s it was estimated that subsidies for energy in OECD countries were running at between $70 billion and $80 billion; their main purpose being to support energy production. Coal is most heavily subsidised, followed by nuclear energy and oil.[7]

Estimates are bound to be imprecise, but it would be reasonable to put the total sums wasted on perverse subsidies in the developed countries at about 3 per cent of their combined GDP—this is equivalent to about 8 per cent of their governments' total spending.

These subsidies are essentially expensive ways of protecting sectoral investments and employment. They are only the most spectacular wastes of government funds, representing entire policies almost all of whose effects on society and the environment are negative. Other government failings are not always so obvious or quantifiable. Sometimes only certain elements of a programme are questionable, or only fractions of public funds may be misdirected or abused. Or government may be carrying out worthwhile activities inefficiently, so that their costs to the taxpayer are higher than necessary. But the net result is that in many of the wealthiest societies that have ever existed in human history, there are still large areas of deprivation, crime rates are high and increasing, health services are plagued by too much demand and occasional scares, and public education sectors seem always to be in crisis. As well, environmental problems are a growing cause for concern at all levels: local, national and global. These problems persist despite very high levels of government spending.

It is this author's view that government's failings arise because many government policies:

• have objectives that are unstated, uncosted, obscure or conflicting;

- reward people, activities or institutions, rather than outcomes; and

- do not reward those who achieve social and environmental goals in ways that are correlated with their effectiveness.

Social Policy Bonds, introduced in the next chapter, aim to deal with these deficiencies.

2

Social Policy Bonds

The previous chapter showed that government interventions in our economies are significant and that, at the very least, many of them are not cost-effective.

Government's performance is in striking contrast to that of the private sector. Deregulation of western economies and lower barriers to trade over the past three decades or so have vastly increased the range and quality of affordable goods and services. The freer operation of self-interest in the private sector has made many individuals very wealthy indeed, and most income earners are better off. But the less well off and unwaged have gained little, at least in relative terms, and people from all backgrounds suffer from what they perceive to be a deteriorating social and physical environment. Many social and environmental objectives remain as remote as ever, despite large—and, in many cases, increasing—sums of taxpayers' money spent on trying to achieve them.

High crime rates, illiteracy, pollution and the threat of climate change, to give some examples, are problems that everyone agrees must be solved. Of course there are differences about priorities, but there is wide consensus that these are problems that deserve attention and some level of government funding for their solution. Where people do disagree is about how to solve them.

Many governments have privatised certain services previously done by national or local government employees. In some countries whole industries have been privatised. Central and local governments have also contracted out services previously done by the public sector: in some US states, allocation of welfare benefits has been so contracted out; while in the UK, hospital laundries, and various other services previously supplied by local authorities have been similarly put out to tender. But the number and range of such contracting-out and privatisation schemes should not obscure the continuing increase in the volume of public spending and the increasing level of government intervention in economic activity. Government is still largely responsible for a whole host of goods, services, transfers and subsidies and investment, and it appears to be performing badly.

The previous chapter hinted that likely sources of the persistence of social and environmental problems are the misstated or conflicting objectives underlying government spending, and the focus of such spending on activities, programmes or institutions, rather than outcomes. The people who are currently charged with solving social problems are generally not rewarded in ways that are correlated with their success in doing so. They might even face disincentives to achieve their supposed objectives. This is not to say that government employees are especially lazy or incompetent. They behave rationally given the incentives they face, but these incentives do not consistently reward the achievement of desired outcomes.

SOCIAL POLICY BONDS

Social Policy Bonds would be a new financial instrument that rewards people only when they actually achieve targeted social or environmental goals. A fixed number of Social Policy Bonds ('bonds') would be issued by local or national government and auctioned to the highest bidders. Government would undertake to redeem these bonds for a fixed sum *only when a specified social objective has been achieved.* The bonds would be freely tradable after issue, and their market value would rise and fall. Social Policy Bonds would therefore differ from conventional bonds in that they would have an uncertain redemption date which, in combination with a fixed redemption value, implies an uncertain yield: holders would raise their bonds' yield by achieving the targeted objective quickly. The bonds would be redeemed from the government's general taxation revenues. The rest of this chapter outlines the essential elements of a bond regime. Subsequent chapters look in more detail at their operational aspects.

How would the Social Policy Bonds work? They would create an interest group—bondholders—who have a strong interest in achieving the targeted social objective efficiently, or in paying others to do so. Consider an example. Assume that an urban authority is prepared to spend a maximum of say $10 million to reduce the crime rate within its borders by 50 per cent. It issues one million bonds that become worth $10 when the crime rate falls below 50 per cent of current levels for a sustained period—say one year. Because the market would see this objective as unlikely to be achieved in the near future, it would put a low value on the bonds when they are floated. Assume successful bidders pay as little as $1 for the bonds. (This sum would be held by the issuing authority partially to offset the cost of future redemption of the bonds.) Now, they hold an asset that could appreciate in value by 900 per cent if a sustained halving of the crime rate were achieved. This provides the motivation for bondholders to do what they can to reduce the crime rate.

Social Policy Bonds could in principle, be used to solve any social or environmental problem that can be reliably defined and quantified. Key criteria for policy areas within which Social Policy Bonds would show the most marked improvement over current programmes are:

1. existing policies have objectives that are unstated, uncosted, obscure or conflicting; and

2. financial rewards to those involved in achieving objectives are uncorrelated to their effectiveness in doing so.

Sadly, there are many such policy areas, including:

- crime prevention,

- employment,

- health,

- education, and

- air, water and noise pollution

HOW MANY BONDS WOULD BE ISSUED?

Before issuing Social Policy Bonds, government would have to decide on the approximate value of the targeted outcome. One consideration would be the financial impact of solving a social problem. Achieving certain social goals would actually bring about financial savings for a government. For instance, the state saves unemployment benefit and gains an increase in income tax for each person who is taken off the unemployment register and goes into gainful employment. Achieving this particular social goal would therefore generate a net fiscal benefit, even in the short term. For other targeted objectives, such as a lower crime rate, there would also be positive, but less easily quantifiable, net financial benefits, and these may take longer to arise. Other social goals, such as reduced rates of homelessness, or increases in literacy, might increase monetary returns to the government in the long term, but would certainly generate very little net revenue in the short run. And there would be many social or environmental goals whose achievement would impose net financial costs on the government in the foreseeable future.

But people and governments want things other than for financial reasons. A society in which everybody can read, in which people feel safer from crime and breathe clean air is surely desirable in its own right. Government and society have to decide on how far we pursue these objectives, and how valuable they are. They would have to take into account both the financial and nonfinancial benefits in deciding on the maximum value of each social goal, in advance of issuing the bonds. A bond regime would make this a simpler and more transparent task than the current array of social policies, because people would be asked to value outcomes, rather than activities intended to achieve these outcomes. If Social Policy Bonds were to be used in conjunction with other policy instruments to achieve the same goal, government would also have to decide on the proportion of total expenditure that would be spent on the bond component. These factors would determine how many bonds it would issue for a definite redemption value. The maximum cost to the government of the bond issue would (ignoring administration costs) equal: the total number of bonds issued multiplied by their redemption value, minus any revenues gained on floating the bonds.

But while it would have to decide on the *maximum* cost to society of achieving the objective, a government issuing Social Policy Bonds would not have to work out how much the *actual* cost would be with any accuracy. That would be done by bidders for the bonds in the open market. Assume again that bonds were to be used exclusively in pursuit of a 50 per cent reduction in the crime rate, and that the urban authority issues one million bonds, of redemption value $10.00. If the market decided that the issue value of these bonds were $1.00, the net cost to the issuers of achieving the targeted objective (ignoring administration costs) would be $9 million. In other words, the market at the time of issue believes that the cost, including its profit margin, of achieving the objective would be $9 million.

But suppose the bond issuers are in the dark about how much it will cost to achieve a targeted objective and instead of issuing one million bonds they issue ten million with the same redemption value, $10.00. They would then be liable for a maximum cost of $100 million. However, the market would still reckon that it could achieve the objective for around $9 million. So instead of valuing the bonds at $1.00 it would bid up the issue price of the bonds to around $9.10. (Social Policy Bonds would be an unusual financial instrument, in that the more

that were issued, the higher would be their value!) *The issuers therefore
would not have to estimate with any accuracy how much a targeted objective might cost to achieve, and they would put a cap on their total liability
by limiting the number of bonds issued.*

So the Social Policy Bond mechanism ensures that the market,
which means people *other than government employees*, would decide
roughly how much it would cost to reach a specified social outcome.
They would do this when they bid for the bonds at issue and at all
times afterwards. This fact, and the would-be bondholders' incentive
to minimise their costs, contrast with the current system in which the
costs of achieving particular outcomes, if they are calculated at all, are
not widely known, nor subject to competitive bidding. Under the current system, in fact, many of the people involved in achieving social
goals have every incentive to inflate the projected cost of their doing so.

Note that the issuing body could add to the number of bonds in circulation after floating at any time, if it wanted to boost the efforts
going into achieving a particular social goal. If it wanted, for whatever
reason, to *reduce* such efforts, the situation would be a little more complicated. It could buy bonds back from holders, but doing so would
reduce the total funds to be spent on achieving the targeted objective,
and so would lower the value of all bonds in circulation. People might
therefore be unwilling to buy bonds in the first place if they thought
there were a high probability of the issuing body's buying some of
them back in this way. They would demand some sort of premium for
taking that risk. Alternatively, the issuing body could undertake either
that it would never buy Social Policy Bonds back or that, if it did, it
would pay the market price ruling before it announced its purchases.

WHAT WOULD BONDHOLDERS DO?

Social Policy Bonds that target the crime rate would rely on the people
or institutions that hold bonds initiating or facilitating crime-reduction programmes. Bondholders could use their own capital, or borrow
on the strength of the redemption value of their bonds. They would

have an incentive to cooperate with each other to help reduce crime, and to do so as cost-effectively as possible. These people's motivation would come from the expected capital gain they would enjoy as the bond price rises in line with the enhanced probability that the objective will be achieved early.

Consider some of the measures that active investors in bonds targeting the crime rate could put into operation:

- encouraging neighbourhood watch schemes;

- encouraging parents to monitor their children's activities more closely;

- subsidising recruitment of unemployed workers; or

- complementing police patrols with private security patrols.

In many countries, some arms of government already undertake one or more of these activities. And some longer-term projects, like research into the causes of crime, are done by private bodies or universities, independently of government or with only a small contribution from government funds. The crucial difference a Social Policy Bond regime would make is that people would have incentives to seek out and develop those ways of reducing crime that are most cost-effective. A police force, a bureaucracy, or an environmental health department, however well-intentioned, is not currently rewarded in ways that correlate with its success in achieving society's objectives—even if these are explicitly targeted. But under a Social Policy Bond regime the self-interest of bondholders would act so as to encourage those ways of reducing crime that would give taxpayers the best return for their outlay. These ways may have been tried before, or tried in different cities, or they may be new and untried. Bondholders would be motivated to seek out, invent and use the most efficient methods for the city or country whose crime rate is targeted.

Bondholders need not participate directly in any crime reduction projects. Their role could be one of financing such projects, on the strength of the redemption value of their bonds, or on the strength of any increase in the value of their bonds. Their motivation would arise from the anticipated supernormal profit arising from early redemption of the bonds.

One further activity that bondholders might indulge in is lobbying government. They might press for longer prison sentences, for example, thinking that these would deter potential criminals or keep convicted criminals out of circulation. Such lobbying, of course, already goes on because government is always making decisions that create winners and losers. Under a Social Policy Bond regime the source of this sort of pressure, and the motivation for it, would be more transparent than under the current system and it need not pose any different problems. The next chapter looks at the subject of lobbying in more detail.

TRADING THE BONDS

Social Policy Bonds, once issued and sold, must be readily tradable at any time until redemption. The operation of such a 'secondary market' would be critical to the way Social Policy Bonds work. Many bond purchasers would want or need to sell their bonds before redemption—which might be a long time in the future. With a secondary market, these holders would be able to realise any capital appreciation experienced by their holdings of Social Policy Bonds whenever they chose to do so. This would make the bonds a more attractive investment in the first place.

Such capital appreciation would arise from upward movements in the market price of the bonds. Of course, these prices could move in either direction. Major determinants of the bond price would be:

- how remote the market believes the targeted objective is to being achieved;

- market perceptions of risk and uncertainty; and

- the relative attractiveness of other investments.

These and other determinants would vary with time. Note that the market's valuation of the bonds would be influenced not only by efforts that bondholders make toward achieving the targeted goal, but by external factors. Some of these could be apparent at the time of issue: for instance, one of the determinants of crime is demography. Specifically, the greater the number of young male adults, the larger the number of crimes tends to be, all other factors being equal. Demographic variables like this, and others that can be anticipated, would be factored into the market value of the bonds at issue. But other influences cannot be anticipated. So, for example, the market price of bonds targeting property crime could fall if, say, there were a string of power failures that led to looting. Or it could rise on the capture of a ringleader of a particularly successful gang of burglars or car thieves. The price of bonds targeting air pollution could rise or fall with climatic conditions, volcanic eruptions, or the price of oil or coal. The value of bonds targeting unemployment could rise or fall with financial data, such as the exchange rate (making the country a more or less attractive venue for overseas investment), or interest rates (making firms more or less likely to lay off employees).

As with other investments, risk and uncertainty would be important determinants of the bonds' market price. Bonds targeting more remote objectives (cutting crime by 80 per cent say) would be riskier than those whose outcomes were closer to current levels (cutting crime by 20 per cent). And there would also be uncertainty attached to the Social Policy Bond mechanism itself, especially in the early years of a bond regime, as it would be untried and unproven.

Like shares and other financial instruments, the prices of Social Policy Bonds would be in constant flux. New information affecting the prices would become available day by day. As well as external influences on the bond prices, people would carry out research aimed at determining the value of the bonds as an investment. The effects of all these data on the bonds' market value would give useful insights into the relationships between circumstances, events, social problems and desired outcomes.

Giving bondholders the chance to benefit from these price movements would be essential. Apart from making the bonds more attractive at issue, a healthy secondary market would be important for another crucial reason: some investors may be able to speed up only one, or a few, of the processes necessary for the targeted objective to be achieved. Once these investors had made their contribution and seen the capital value of their bonds increase in line with the increased probability of the bonds' early redemption, they might have no wish to speculate on the speed at which the remaining processes would be carried out. Other groups of active investors, who could have greater expertise in performing these later processes, must be given an incentive to use their expertise to accelerate attainment of the targeted objective. The possible capital appreciation of bonds bought from previous owners and sold at a still higher price (or redeemed) would provide this incentive. The new owners would, if they were successful in these later stages, realise this capital appreciation.

CASCADING INCENTIVES

As the bonds were traded, they would tend to flow towards those who were most able to help solve the targeted social problem. In fact, though, trading in the bonds would not always have to occur. Large bondholders might simply decide to subcontract out the required work to many different agents, while they themselves would hold the bonds from issue to redemption. The important point is that the bond mechanism would ensure that the people who allocate the finance had an incentive to do so efficiently and to reward successful outcomes, rather than merely to pay people for undertaking an activity. At the limit just one single investor could buy all the bonds. If this buyer were determined to hold on to the bonds until redemption, then the bonds would function as a sort of performance-related contract, with the issuers paying only when the objective had been achieved. The buyer could contract out most, or all, of the work required to achieve the objective, with the incentives generated by the bonds for speedy accomplishment cascading down from the bondholder to those subcontracted to do the work. If this bondholder, for whatever reason, were to become inefficient in pursuit of that objective, or were simply to lose interest in it, then he or she could simply sell the bonds to more efficient and more highly motivated investors.

Too large a number of small bondholders would probably do little to help solve targeted social problems by themselves. If there were many small holders, it is likely that the value of their bonds would fall until there were aggregation of holdings by people or institutions large enough to initiate effective problem-solving projects. In much the same way as share privatisation issues the world over have turned out, the bonds might end up mainly in the hands of large holders, be they individuals or institutions. Between them, these large holders could account for the majority of bond holding. Even these bodies might not be big enough, on their own, to achieve much without the cooperation of other bondholders. They might also resist initiating projects until they could be sure that other holders would not be 'free riders' (see the next chapter). So there would be a powerful incentive for all bondholders to *cooperate with each other* to help solve the targeted problem. They would share the same interest in seeing targeted objectives achieved quickly. So they would share information, trade bonds with each other and collaborate on objective-achieving projects. They would also set up payment systems to ensure that people, bondholders or not, were mobilised to help achieve targeted objectives. Bondholders would either trade bonds, or make incentive payments to ensure that any proceeds from higher bond prices, or from redemption, would be channelled in ways most likely to stimulate speedy achievement of the targeted objective. Large bondholders, in cooperation with each other, would be able to set up such systems cost-effectively.

Regardless of who actually owns the bonds, aggregation of holdings and the cooperation of large bondholders would ensure that people who help achieve social goals were rewarded in ways that maximise their efficiency.

OBJECTIVES AND INDICATORS

For a Social Policy Bond regime to be effective, clarity and transparency of objectives would be essential. The targeted objective must be *carefully defined* so that targeted changes either actually are, or are strongly correlated with, what society wants to achieve. For instance, numbers of reported crimes could be targeted if the objective were to achieve a safer urban environment. But this indicator may be unsatisfactory if, for instance, the crime rate became so high that people did not bother to report minor assaults or burglaries to the police. A more appropriate indicator might be derived from responses to victim surveys. Because the bonds target outcomes they demand clear thinking and transparency as to exactly what it is that society is aiming to achieve. Is lower unemployment the objective? Or lower expenditure on unemployment benefit? Or higher employment? Is it worthwhile aiming to reduce, in particular, unemployment amongst 16–24 year old males? Or ethnic minorities? Or the unemployment rate in particular regions? Also note that it would clearly be unsatisfactory to redeem the bonds the moment a targeted fall in unemployment had been achieved. The objective should be a *sustained* lower level of unemployment, and that is how it would have to be defined when the bonds were issued.

Targeted objectives should also be capable of being *targeted by quantifiable indicators*, whose progress accurately corresponds with progress toward the desired social outcome. As well, objectives should, in general, be as *broad* as possible, so that one particular objective cannot be achieved at the expense of other societal goals.

The last point needs elaboration. Consider the application of a bond regime to environmental problems. Assume the concentration of atmospheric lead were to be targeted by a bond issue. It might be that targeting lead in this way would cause people to increase their use of other polluting substitutes—and these could be at least as dangerous as the original levels of lead.

One way of dealing with this problem could be to aim initially at an unambitious reduction in the lead level. Depending on the effects of such a reduction on the use of offending substitutes, other bonds could then be issued, either targeting the level of lead, or targeting the level of offending substitutes. But a better approach would be to target, more comprehensively, atmospheric pollution. This could be expressed perhaps as an index of atmospheric pollutants, weighted according to their lethality and other factors (see box, *What to target?*).

What to target?

Breadth of objective Targeted objectives should, in principle, be as broad as possible. It would probably be unsatisfactory to make nitrates, for example, the sole target of a bond issue targeting water pollution if it were likely that farmers would respond by increasing the use of phosphates. Instead, both could be made the target of a single bond issue or, even better, water pollution itself could be targeted: Social Policy Bonds lend themselves to targeting combinations of objectives. They could target indices encompassing a wide range of pollutants, weighted according to their contribution to environmental degradation.

Ends or means? In principle ends, rather than means to ends, would make better targets for Social Policy Bonds. Thus, it would be preferable for bond issuers to target, for example, homelessness, rather than housing starts, and leave it for bondholders to decide on how best to achieve the desired goal. Similarly, it might be preferable to target not water pollution, but such indicators of environmental status as biodiversity of a river, lake or sea, perhaps in conjunction with more subjective indicators like the views people have about the quality of their environment, as measured by questionnaire responses. Bonds could be issued whose redemption value were on a sliding scale, reflecting the perceived adverse environmental impacts of the targeted range of pollutants.

Spatial distribution Bonds aimed at improving national averages of such
indicators as pollution would be adequate sole policy instruments only if
society were unconcerned about the distribution of pollutants. Otherwise
bonds targeting pollution could be made redeemable only on the condition
that pollutant thresholds would not breached in any part of the country
concerned.

Time period Bond issues could provide bonus payments for achievement of
the targeted goal by a specified date. Or issuers could stipulate that bonds
would not be redeemed unless the targeted objective were achieved by a
certain date, or that they would be redeemed for a sum that would diminish
over the time it took for the objective to be achieved. The market would factor
all such penalties or bonuses into the bond price.

Similar concerns, perhaps less clear-cut, could arise when targeting
regional problems. If bonds were issued targeting the number of unemployed people of working age in northeast England, say, then bondholders might attempt to solve the problem by paying the unemployed
of that region to move somewhere else. This might, of course, be seen
as a social benefit. But if not, provisos could written into the bond
issue, such that they would not be redeemed if the population in the
north-east fell below a certain level. In general, objectives that are complementary and that, if not pursued jointly, could conflict, should be
targeted by a single bond issue.

3

Practicalities and potential problems

Social Policy Bonds would represent a radical change in the way in which our society does things. At first sight, a bond regime may even seem outlandish: it would appear to mean government giving up its responsibility for achieving social goals to the private sector. It would also allow private companies to profit from the public purse. But it is important to realise that under a Social Policy Bond regime government would merely be contracting out the *achievement* of social objectives. Government would still set these goals and, by undertaking to redeem the bonds, would still be the ultimate source of finance for the projects that achieve them. Moreover, competitive bidding for bonds would bid away excessive company profits. People would need to be reminded of these facts when asked to contemplate a bond regime. Nevertheless, the concept does raise some important questions. Could free riders undermine operation of a bond regime? Could a bond regime generate perverse financial incentives? This chapter begins by looking at these questions, then goes on to consider other practical aspects of a Social Policy Bond regime.

THE FREE RIDER QUESTION

Many people might purchase Social Policy Bonds with the idea of doing nothing but holding on to them until they could sell them at a profit. Such passive investors would have no intention of doing anything to help achieve the social goal targeted by their bonds. Some of

them could be casual purchasers who would buy the bonds with the
same intent as they would a lottery ticket. They would hope to hold
bonds until their redemption, or until their market value had risen suf-
ficiently high for them to enjoy a worthwhile capital gain. Other passive investors might be speculators who thought that the likelihood of
the targeted objective being achieved quickly were greater than the rest
of the market believed it to be—in other words, that the bonds were
underpriced.

Another category of passive investor might be the hedger. These
would be people who, in the absence of the bond issue, would stand to
lose if the particular targeted objective were achieved. Hedgers might
buy the bonds as a form of insurance against that possibility. If crime
were targeted, for example, hedgers might be those who breed guard
dogs, for instance, or glaziers who operate where street crime is preva-
lent. (Actually, though, the losers from particular Social Policy Bond
issues might not be clearly identifiable in advance, because the bonds
would not stipulate *how* a goal is to be achieved. So, bondholders
might decide that one of the most effective ways of reducing crime
would be to subsidise the cost of guard dogs to home owners, which
would *increase* demand for the animals.)

Casual purchasers and speculators would want to become 'free riders', hoping to benefit from any increase in the bond price without
actually participating in any objective-achieving projects. Hedgers
wouldn't particularly want the value of their bonds to rise, but their
bondholding would similarly reduce the supply of bonds available to
active investors. None of these passive purchasers of Social Policy
Bonds would do much to help achieve targeted goals. However, markets for the bonds would work to limit the benefits from passive investing. To see this, assume that most of a particular issue of bonds were
held by would-be free riders. Then very little, if anything, would be
done to help achieve the targeted objective. As the objective became
more remote, the value of all the bonds would fall. And as the bonds
lost value, they would make a more attractive purchase for people who

were prepared actively to help achieve the targeted objective. So free riders would be tempted to sell, even at a loss, rather than see the value of their bonds continue to fall. Some history of falling bond prices would tend to make free riding on Social Policy Bonds less appealing with future issues. Free riding then would become a self-cancelling activity. There are other reasons why bondholding would be unattractive to potential free riders:

- Individual free riders would have no incentive to collude with other free riders, because the more they did so, the more remote the targeted objective would become, and the further would the value of their bonds fall. This would act so as to limit any free riding activity to small players.

- As with other financial instruments, small players would have to pay higher transaction costs than the bigger institutions—the ones that would be most likely to initiate objective-achieving projects.

- Small players also would not have access to the research that would enable big players to value the bonds accurately. Therefore they would be at a disadvantage in the market.

Note also that even if free riders were to gain from holding Social Policy Bonds, they would do be doing so only because their bonds had risen in value as a result of a targeted objective becoming closer to being achievement. As well, attempted free riding would have positive effects: it would add liquidity to the bond market.

In short, there are grounds to believe that free riding would not seriously undermine the operation of a Social Policy Bond regime, mainly because it is unlikely much free riding would occur, and partly because even if it did occur, it would not impede the operation of the bond mechanism

PERVERSE INCENTIVES

Assume that a national government issues Social Policy Bonds targeting air pollution. Bondholders might then try to persuade or bribe polluting firms to reduce their emissions. But what if polluters spurned
bondholders' blandishments and continued to pollute at the same
level? Bond prices would therefore fall, and polluters could collude to
buy them at a lower price. They would then profit by reducing pollution and redeeming their bonds. If a pattern of such behaviour were
established, would not polluters then be the only investors in future
issues of bonds targeting pollution? A quick answer would point out
that the targeted objective would still have been achieved for a sum
equal to, or less than, the maximum cost for which the issuers have
allowed. True, the cost would be lower if there were no such collusion.
But another answer is that bonds are only one weapon in a government's armoury. Regulation of pollution, or the threat of it, would
work to raise the market value of the bonds, and make such behaviour
risky. This type of behaviour would probably be a threat only when
there were a few big polluters who could collude. (In such circumstances a bond regime might anyway not be the best pollution control
mechanism, because their informational advantages over tradable permits for example (see chapter 4) might not be so significant.) But what
if, following a bond issue, businesses were to pollute *more* than they
otherwise would, and gain from bondholders paying them to stop? In
effect they would pollute more on the expectation they would receive
enhanced payment for reducing pollution in the future. This behaviour would also, however, have some risk attached, because bondholders might calculate that the most cost-effective reductions could be
achieved by businesses other than such anti-social polluters, or that the
objective could be achieved in other ways such as, for example, removing air pollutants from the atmosphere. If pollution were a by-product
of production, then the output of these polluters would be at an above-
optimal quantity, so their pollution increase would not be costless.

But the possibility still arises that these businesses could profit from such behaviour. Or even that people who previously generated no pollution whatsoever might begin to pollute so that they could benefit either from bondholders' paying them to pollute less, or from buying pollution control bonds cheaply, and then reducing their pollution and selling their bonds at a higher price. In all these cases there need be no collusion amongst bondholders. For 'market fundamentalists' contemplating using Social Policy Bonds as the sole means of achieving social and environmental goals, this might constitute a fatal flaw. But, again, the bonds would almost certainly complement a government's regulatory powers—including its powers to make new regulations and charge companies on the basis of how much pollution they emit. In such instances there would probably be enough existing or potential legal (and moral) sanction against cynical polluters to ensure that it need not happen. Governments would certainly retain its powers to tax or regulate in ways that would make perverse increases in pollution more risky, or criminal. And it bears repeating that, in a bond regime, bondholders would have powerful incentives to see that any existing rules against pollution were enforced, or that new and effective regulations on polluters would be imposed.

Nevertheless, and more generally, Social Policy Bonds would work by generating financial incentives for people to achieve particular goals, and this might encourage people to break the law to do so. Examples of acts that would be illegal, but that certain bond issues might encourage, are:

- emitting pollutants that, while unspecified in bonds targeting pollution, were still controlled or banned;

- forcibly preventing people from registering as unemployed, if bonds targeting unemployment were issued; or

- falsifying data used to compile measures of longevity or infant mortality that were elements of a targeted health objective.

Acts such as these are already illegal and will continue to be so, but before issuing Social Policy Bonds governments should be aware that there would be greater inducements to commit them. Bondholders would need reassurance that government would not relinquish its existing sanctions against illegal activities.

The bonds might also induce people to modify behaviour in ways that, while not illegal, would undermine what they were trying to achieve. So, for example, if bonds targeting the number of reported property crimes were issued, bondholders might lobby insurance companies not to insist on police reports before paying out. Or they might persuade, or pay, insurance companies to raise their excess levels. Either activity would discourage people from reporting minor thefts. Neither would do anything to reduce property crime, but they would each make the targeted objective, lower numbers of *reported* property crimes, more achievable, and so lead to a rise in the bonds' market value. Insurance companies themselves could own the bonds, and so it would be in their own interest to deter people from reporting property crimes. In this particular case, the objective could be more carefully specified so as to target not 'reported crimes' but, for instance, the number of people who, in surveys of the public, say that they have experienced property crimes.

If higher levels of literacy were targeted, bondholders may be tempted to lobby in favour of easier reading tests. Again, judicious specification of the targeted objective would help: the bonds could stipulate the exact reading test to be used, or that the test would have to be certified as appropriate by a specified panel of impartial literacy experts.

In general though, carefully specified objectives might not always eliminate or mitigate the kind of illegal, or negative-but-legal, activities that the bonds may stimulate. So how could this potential problem be solved? A first response would be to point out that negative effects of policies occur nowadays, and that in today's political environment policymakers and officials can escape or deflect censure because the adverse results of their policies are difficult to relate to their cause. If Social Policy Bonds were to lead to negative effects, the relationship between these effects and their cause would be easier to identify, and deterring such effects would be simpler than doing so under the current activity—or institutional—based funding arrangements. But a more considered response would look more closely at the role of government in a bond regime, and at the way in which the bonds could be introduced.

INTRODUCTION OF A SOCIAL POLICY BOND REGIME

Social Policy Bonds would need to be introduced cautiously. They should be tried out on an experimental basis at first. Initial goals could be relatively small scale and uncontroversial, and the bonds could complement, rather than replace, existing government or local authority programmes. Amongst the first targeted objectives could be petty crime in particular cities, or the amount of litter deposited on city streets, or illiteracy rates of schoolchildren or adults. Local authorities could also issue bonds that target the water quality in rivers, for instance; indicators of success could be the number and variety of fish present. Unemployment amongst racial minorities, or in particular cities, could also be early targets of a Social Policy Bond regime. Such contained, easily identifiable goals would help the bonds gain acceptability amongst the public, and encourage policymakers to discuss and refine the concept. Watching out for negative behaviour of, or on behalf of, holders of such locally issued bonds would be a fairly simple matter. And if local authorities issued bonds in tranches, targeting incremental improvements in indicators, observing and remedying any negative behaviour would be even simpler. Later tranches of bonds could incorporate provisos stipulating that they would be redeemed only if any unwanted, and previously untargeted, activities did not exceed a minimal level.

Bond issuing authorities would apply lessons learned from such trials to different bond issues, while central government could collate and apply these lessons before issuing bonds with national application.

When bonds targeted new objectives for the first time they would be especially likely to encourage unanticipated negative behaviour by bondholders. Lessons learned from such initial issues could be applied to later issues targeting the same objective. These lessons would extend beyond how to deal with bondholders' behaviour. They might, for instance, give some direction as to the circumstances under which bonds could best be used as complements to existing policies, and when they could safely replace them.

A cautious, gradual, introduction of Social Policy Bonds would be one means of minimising potential problems of a bond regime. If, despite such an approach, bondholders behaved illegally, government could prosecute the perpetrators. And if bondholders behaved in negative, but legal ways, government would have other options. In ascending order of severity, government could:

- persuade or cajole bondholders into toeing the line. It could do this publicly or privately—initially, at least, bondholdings could be registered in the same way as shares;

- buy back bonds, which would have the effect of lowering the market price of bonds remaining on the market (by reducing the total redemption funds; see chapter 2);

- legislate against the negative activity; or

- declare the bonds null and void, and offer compensation related to the bonds' issue price or their current market price.

EFFECTS ON GOVERNMENT'S BEHAVIOUR

Another possible problem arising from the integration of Social Policy Bonds into the current policy-making system arises from government's role as creator of statutes. This was mentioned fleetingly in chapter 2 in connection with holders of bonds targeting crime, who might think it worthwhile to lobby government for longer prison sentences. Government has the power to pass laws that would affect bond prices, or its actions could influence bond prices in other ways. For instance: government could come under great pressure not to increase unemployment benefits from holders of bonds targeting the number of registered unemployed. Note, though, that the source of the pressure, and the motivation for it, would be easy to identify. And lobbying is a legitimate activity. There is no reason why bondholders, in common with other pressure groups, should not lobby politicians. They would be doing so mainly out of financial self-interest of course. But existing pressure groups are also self-interested, and in the case of bondholders their self-interest would be more likely to coincide with society's interests if targeted objectives were correctly specified. Bondholders would lobby for legislative change, and they would benefit in obvious, pecuniary ways if they were successful.

When they assess the value of the bonds, potential investors would take into account such possible changes in legislation and their potential influence on the speed at which the targeted objective could be achieved. These influences would though make it important for there to be some element of consultation when selecting targeted objectives. People become wealthy by exerting influence on politicians under the current system, but they and their effects on behaviour are not always identifiable. As now, under a bond regime it would be up to politicians to weigh the evidence for and against any course of action promoted by lobbyists, with due regard to the lobbyists' motivation. And it would be up to potential investors in Social Policy Bonds to take into account likely or possible changes in the legislative environment when bidding for the bonds.

The threat of bondholders lobbying governments for legislative changes could have a positive aspect. For bond issues to be as successful as possible, governments would ideally give assurances as to their future behaviour. These could mean making relatively simple decisions early on. They might, for instance, decide now on the type of reading test to be used to determine literacy in a decade's time. But they could also

choose to be more definite about their long-term spending plans. Take
bonds targeting national crime rates: would-be bondholders would be
very interested to know as much as possible about government's projected expenditures on policing. Similarly, prospective purchasers of
bonds targeting atmospheric pollution would want to know, for
instance, the government's petrol taxation, electricity generation or
road building plans. Government would maximise interest in the
bonds by being as open about its legislative and spending intentions as
soon as possible. Government could also undertake *not* to do such
things as reduce police numbers—such assurances would doubtless be
subject to the usual scepticism attending pronouncements of this type.

The question of government behaviour can be seen in a different
light. Government, as well as bondholders and society in general,
would want Social Policy Bonds to be successful. Its assurances about
its legislative and spending plans will never be absolute, but by giving
what assurances it could a government would enhance the market for
the bonds, and be able to achieve more social goals with the same budget. One way that a government issuing Social Policy Bonds could do
this would be for it to specify that, as far as possible, its behaviour
would be determined by objective criteria. So government might
declare to potential investors in bonds targeting unemployment, for
example, that changes in unemployment benefit payments would be
strictly related to movements in a retail price index.

Of course, if the bonds were to target only small changes in unemployment, or crime rates, or air pollution, or whatever, the government's long-range plans would not be so significant to prospective
bondholders. Targeting incremental improvements in social indicators,
it might emerge after trials of the bond concept, could be the best way
of dealing with the uncertainties of future government behaviour.
Alternatively there may be many social goals for which it turns out that
government's behaviour is a relatively insignificant component of the
uncertainty that attaches to investment in any financial instrument:

markets routinely deal with uncertainty by attaching lower values to riskier instruments.

While government's assurances about its future behaviour would exercise investors' minds, they would also be important to people who are consumers of government services. There would be important implications for bonds that target welfare expenditure. Take for example Social Policy Bonds that, aiming to tackle unemployment, would be redeemed only when spending on unemployment benefit fell by a certain level. Bondholders would then have an incentive to discourage people from applying for, or continuing to receive, unemployment benefit. They might lobby government not to increase the unemployment benefit paid to each person on the unemployment register, or even to reduce it. While it is difficult to imagine bondholders' doing so, and thereby incurring the wrath of much of the rest of society, there are no compelling reasons for making such lobbying illegal. But where government *should* draw the line, firmly, is on the question of who decides whether or not a person qualifies for state benefits. Decisions as to eligibility for state benefits must remain with the state. This is mainly for ethical reasons: these benefits are set, ultimately, by the political process, and are anyway little more than a safety net for most recipients. Bondholders should have the right to provide alternatives to these benefits; even to pay people not to claim them. But they should not have the right to decide who should qualify for them.

ASSESSMENT OF INDICATORS AND INSIDER TRADING

A bond regime would rely on authoritative, accurate and timely monitoring of the targeted social or environmental problem so that progress towards its solution could be impartially assessed. There would probably be private sector information gathering, but the definitive, official, figures would have to be seen to be independent of bondholders, who could benefit unfairly from dubious data collection. Naturally the information as to how close the objective were to being achieved would have value. It would not be difficult, for instance, to imagine the latest official unemployment figures being sought in advance of official publication and used for 'insider trading' of bonds targeting unemployment If too much insider trading went on, it would increase the riskiness of the bonds to those without access to this information and tarnish their value as an investment. So how could it be minimised?

- Those involved in gathering, collating and processing relevant data could be bound by terms deterring or forbidding them from abusing privileged information.

- If large sums of money were at stake, there would be a great deal of private information gathering: investors, bondholders, and financial commentators would take their own soundings throughout the lifetime of each bond issue. There would be more interest in more frequently updated information, so that progress toward achieving objectives could be more readily charted. All this would serve to remove some of the allure from privileged figures that had yet to be publicised.

- Indicators for targeted objectives could be chosen with a view to minimising the possibility of insider trading being an important factor. Some imprecision about how objectives would be measured would help: a government could stipulate that bonds targeting such objectives as urban atmospheric pollution or crime rates in cities would be redeemed on the basis of data from a random sample of cities, rather than from all cities or a predetermined set of cities.

- The objectives themselves could be chosen to minimise the possibility of insider trading. Bonds targeting long-range objectives, such as cutting crime rates or unemployment by 50 per cent rather than 10 per cent, would probably be less sensitive to insider trading. With long-range objectives, each datum illegally withheld from the bond market would probably represent a smaller proportion of the total relevant information available to the bond market, and so have a lesser effect on the bond's market value.

None of these ways of mitigating insider trading would always be fully effective. That said, there are already sensitive indicators, such as unemployment or retail sales figures, that are capable of moving markets, and so there are already in place mechanisms to keep such information secret until it is time for publication. There are also sanctions against those who obtain, and act on, such information illegally. These mechanisms and sanctions might need to be strengthened under a bond regime, but it remains to be seen how important abuse of insider information would be. While insider trading does mean that unscrupulous people benefit at the expense of the public, it does not generally impede the operation of markets. Markets continue to function and the possibility that a low level of insider trading goes on is generally discounted by the broader market.

FUTURES AND OPTIONS MARKETS

Another possible source of perverse incentives could arise from the development of futures and options markets in Social Policy Bonds. These would enable people to benefit from a falling bond price, so giving them an incentive to delay achievement of the targeted goal.

It is quite likely that there would be futures and options markets for large bond issues, and it is almost certain that the price of any particular Social Policy Bond would not always be increasing along an upward trend from its float price to its redemption value. It would be justifiable, as well as efficient, if bondholders could hedge against consequent falls in the value of their assets. People who do not hold bonds might want to participate in markets for derivatives of bonds, some of which would rise in value as the targeted goal became more remote. This in turn means that speculators and short sellers could certainly profit from *short-term* bond price falls, and the question is whether these people would then take steps to impede progress towards any targeted goal.

There are two main reasons why they would probably not. The first is that, in the long term, the weight of money would be against them.

Provided sufficient funds were allocated to achieving the targeted objective, there would be a net positive sum of money payable if the targeted objective were to be achieved, and a net zero sum paid as long as the goal were not achieved. All the long-term incentive would be to achieve the targeted objective. Those who, for whatever reason, would suffer from achievement of the objective could be compensated by bondholders, or bribed to change their ideas. Note also that for every buyer of a 'put' option there would be a seller, and that for every futures contract *bought* on the expectation that the bond price would fall, there would be an equivalent futures contract *sold* on that basis, so that the net incentive generated by derivatives would be in line with the incentive created by the underlying financial instrument, the Social Policy Bond: in the long run, this would favour achievement of the targeted objective.

The other reason that short sellers, or holders of put options, in Social Policy Bonds might not take actions aimed at interfering with achievement of the goal is that such actions might well already be illegal or, again given the incentives that the bonds would generate, be made illegal once the bonds had been issued.

GOVERNMENT AS PURCHASER OF BONDS

Government agencies could, as competitive suppliers of objective-achieving services, participate as active investors in Social Policy Bonds under certain conditions. Unlike in industry the private sector would be unlikely to cry 'unfair competition', even if the operations of these agencies were heavily subsidised, because its own bonds would appreciate as a result of the government, or government-inspired, activity.

If government agencies were to participate in the Social Policy Bond market, they should not have privileged access to information. Also, it is important that any profits they receive, or losses that they incur as a result should accrue to that agency. The people who work for government agencies must have the same incentives as private sector bodies to perform efficiently. This would change the character of these agencies, and would probably lead to their ultimate divorce from the public sector.

EXISTING INSTITUTIONS AND THE TRANSITION TO A SOCIAL POLICY BOND REGIME

Few bodies charged with achieving social goals are currently paid in ways that encourage better performance. Nevertheless these bodies are the main sources of expertise for solving social problems and some of them are bound to be efficient, or to be capable of becoming efficient, in doing so. It would be unwise as well as unfair and unnecessary to cut their funding too severely. The answer, at least for goals in policy areas for which there are already significant institutions, would be a gradual transition.

Take health, for example. In the UK, central government provides funding for health authorities (for spending on doctors, hospitals and prescriptions) according mainly to population level, age and need. Government also supplies funds directly to medical research organisations and academic institutions. A transition to an outcome-based, rather than institution—or activity—based, funding programme would see the funds from government gradually decline, while expenditure allocated from holders of Social Policy Bonds to the outcomes that these institutions are collectively trying to achieve—longer life spans and a better quality of life, say—would gradually rise.

On introducing such a bond regime a government could decide to reduce its funding of health authorities and research institutes by 1 per cent a year, in real terms. (The government could allocate the saved funding to the future redemption of the health bonds it has issued.) So after five years, each health authority would be receiving directly from central government only 95 per cent of the funding that it formerly received. But bondholders could choose to supplement the income of some of these health bodies. They may judge a particular group of health authorities to be especially effective at converting the funds they receive into measurable health benefits, as defined by their bonds' redemption terms. Particularly effective health authorities are likely to be working in deprived areas, where small outlays typically bring about larger improvements in health. Or bondholders might judge a particular research body to be worthy of additional funding, because it was conducting excellent research into a condition that would be likely to respond especially effectively, in terms of health outcomes, to additional expenditure. In such cases, bondholders would supplement their selected health authorities' or research institutes' funding. It may well be that these favoured bodies end up receiving considerably more than their former income throughout the lifetime of a bond regime.

It could also happen that investors in bonds targeting health look at completely new ways of achieving health objectives; ways that currently receive no, or very little, funding. To give a not entirely unbelievable example, they may be convinced that one of the best ways of achieving society's health objectives is to deter teenagers from driving. Following this logic, they may find that one of the most efficient ways of doing would be to lay on subsidised taxis for teenagers attending parties. It is difficult to imagine how our current activity—or institution—based government fund allocation mechanisms could decide on such a programme. More generally, it is quite likely that holders of bonds targeting health outcomes would greatly expand funding in areas such as health education or preventive medicine that rely on expertise outside those bodies traditionally devoted to health care.

Could bonds targeting remote objectives, such as increasing longevity significantly, or reducing the crime rate by half, be compatible with a gradual transition of the type described above, where funding to existing health institutions reduces by 1 per cent annually? At first sight there would be an apparent mismatch between such incremental reductions in government spending and the time scale needed to reach long-range objectives. The critical point here is that bondholders would be investing not on the basis of the annual reductions in government expenditure on existing health institutions, but on the basis of the redemption value of all the bonds issued. To be more precise, it would be this total redemption value, minus the bonds' existing market value, that would inform bondholders' investment decisions. This sum could be many times each year's incremental reduction in government's institution-based spending. One of the virtues of a Social Policy Bond regime is that *even in the short term bondholders would begin to invest in projects with a long range objective* on the expectation of capital gains that might arise only in the distant future.

The accumulated reductions in spending to existing institutions would be one, but not the only, factor influencing how much government decides to spend on achieving a specified social goal. Also important would be the financial savings (if any) that achieving the objective would bring about, and the value society would place on any nonfinancial benefits.

Similarly gradual transitions would be warranted in other areas, such as education and crime, where schools and police forces, some of which are bound to be much more effective than others, are well entrenched. These institutions would receive slowly diminishing absolute levels of funding directly from government, while bondholders would again focus their spending on especially rewarding, in terms of specified education and crime outcomes, projects and institutions. As with health, it is likely that those areas that are initially most disadvantaged would again provide bondholders with the greatest return per unit outlay.

In newer policy areas, particularly the environment, it may be possible to expand spending allocated via the bonds at a faster rate: expertise in the environment is still relatively mobile, and it would be easier to quickly establish new outcome-based institutions or to reorientate existing ones.

INTERACTION WITH EXISTING PROGRAMMES AND PROJECTS

Note that, while changes in the source of funds would be gradual, those involved in existing institutions may well react by quickly reviewing how *all* their existing programmes and projects operate. If bondholders saw existing programmes as being particularly effective in achieving targeted outcomes, then they would be inclined to invest in them. On the one hand, the switch in funding would warn existing institutions that they could expect to see their relatively ineffective operations receive diminishing funds in the future. On the other hand, their effective operations could look forward to higher—possibly much higher—funding. Even a gradual transition involving 1 per cent annual cuts in funds allocated to existing institutions that was balanced by a bond issue could bring about a rapid change in the way existing bodies conducted all their programmes. They may have to devote some of their resources into persuading bondholders of the cost-effectiveness of their activities; but this would not represent a radical difference from the way these bodies lobby for government funding nowadays. Under a bond regime they would have to do their lobbying on a more transparent, outcome-oriented, basis.

WOULD GOVERNMENTS PLAY FAIR?

Might issuing governments themselves try to avoid redeeming Social Policy Bonds, either by reneging on their commitments to do so, or by doing what they could to stop targeted goals from being achieved? The answer is: probably not. If governments were to issue Social Policy Bonds, they would be doing so as representatives of their citizens. They would therefore be under strong moral pressure to comply with their commitment to supply funds for bond redemption, and not to take actions impeding progress toward the targeted goal. But it would also be in governments' own interest to fulfil their obligations. If they did not, they would be discrediting the entire bond principle, which they might well want to deploy again, either domestically or as participants in efforts to solve global social or environmental problems.

WHAT HAPPENS ONCE AN OBJECTIVE HAS BEEN ACHIEVED?

Once an objective were close to achievement, the issuing body could float a new set of Social Policy Bonds aimed at maintaining the achieved outcome or at further improvements. Sustaining the outcome beyond the period specified in the original bond issue would probably be cheaper than achieving it, while further improvements targeted by a second bond issue would most likely cost less, in terms of benefit per unit outlay, than those achieved by the first issue. There are three main reasons for this, the first two of which are linked:

1. Assume that a bond issue aimed at reducing the level of some indi-
    cator from x led to its reaching a level of y. Most probably it would
    take more than a withdrawal of this funding for the indicator to
    revert back to x. Why? If the indicator represents the rate, in per
    cent, of unemployment in one area, for example, many of the
    newly employed would stay in work, even if the absence of further
    expenditure on a bond issue meant that their salary would revert to
    the level that had previously failed to attract them into work. This
    would be partly because they were now more aware of the existence
    of low-paid work, partly because of the costs and disruption of
    reverting to an unemployed lifestyle and partly because they would
    now find the prospect of being unemployed less attractive than
    previously. If the indicator represented air pollution, to take
    another example, maintaining lower levels of pollution could be
    cheaper than achieving it because people would have invested in
    machinery or other systems that cost less, per unit benefit, to keep
    running than they did to set up.

2. In a similar fashion, investors in Social Policy Bonds would learn
    from their experience of achieving the objective targeted by the
    first bond issue. They would have looked for, and experimented
    with, different methods of solving the targeted social problem, and
    would be able to choose the most efficient solutions for subsequent
    bond issues. If maintaining the cleanliness of a river, for instance,
    were targeted, then it is likely that any know-how about monitor-
    ing systems or equipment installation would be more cheaply

available once an initial targeted lower level had already been achieved.

3. Less specifically, it is likely that general improvements in productivity, mainly arising from technology (including information technology), will continue to occur in our economies, and that bondholders would make use of them.

Of course, new issues of Social Policy Bonds might not be the most cost-effective way of maintaining the achieved outcome. There might well be circumstances in which alternative government actions, such as legislation or institutional monitoring, could be preferable.

CONCLUSION

The introduction of a Social Policy Bond regime would be accompanied by operational challenges and problems, not all of which can be anticipated. But these potential problems should not be overstated. Existing laws, careful choice and specification of targeted objectives, more transparency in government as to what it wants to achieve and how it will behave would probably circumvent or remedy most of them. And some of the problems that a bond regime would entail are the inevitable result of policies that have as their measure of achievement quantifiable indicators. In an increasingly complex and interlinked world, the trend toward using these indicators for policymaking purposes is likely to continue, regardless of whether Social Policy Bonds are issued or not. The broader point is that the likely performance of a bond regime needs to be compared with current policymaking methods.

4

Advantages of a Social Policy Bond regime

This chapter looks at some of the likely advantages of Social Policy Bonds over current policies. The chapter concludes with a look at how a bond regime with the objective of climate stability could improve on the Kyoto Protocol.

EFFICIENCY

The main likely advantage of Social Policy Bonds is that, because they would inject self-interest into all stages necessary for solving social problems, they would be *more cost-effective* than current, activity-based programmes. For the same government expenditure, therefore, more could be achieved.

Social Policy Bonds would inject incentives into all activities currently undertaken to bring about social goals. This overarching source of efficiency was looked at in chapter 2. But one consequence of it deserves more consideration here: the encouragement a bond regime would give to investigate new activities and experiment with different activities in different regions.

Government has real difficulties in investigating new approaches in its social and environmental programmes. This is partly because government is generally more interested in preventing failure than in rewarding success. In many areas of social and environmental policy it believes it should carry out only those activities that it can plausibly justify on the basis of a past record. These need not be very efficient, or even partly efficient. As far as many government bodies are concerned they need only to have been tried in the past and not to have been publicly identified as disastrous. This is not a strategy designed to optimise performance; rather it is a strategy that minimises the perceived risk of failure. It leads to the continuing of inefficient, unimaginative activities, whose main recommendation is that they have been done before. As the persistence of social problems attests, these activities are not always very successful.

Neither can government readily try different ideas in different regions, partly because then it would have to face criticism from people who had experienced the less successful ideas. So government generally adopts a uniform approach. In some policy areas, such as education or the environment, it is too easy for central government to override the wishes of local authorities, while local authorities themselves are tempted to override the policies of, say, individual schools or private property owners when it comes to education or environmental matters. But smaller policymaking bodies, be they local government, individual schools or private property owners, often want to employ diverse approaches, and these approaches might well be optimally efficient *in the local circumstances* at achieving desired outcomes.

In one area, for example, crime might be a very obvious and direct result of unemployment. A factory closure might be expected to lead to a soaring crime rate in one particular locality where, perhaps, young males would be put out of work. But under most countries' crime-reduction regimes there is very little incentive for anyone to explore this link and see whether diverting funds from, say, the police to employment creation on a small scale, would be a better way of fighting crime. Most governments would find it politically difficult to subsidise the continued operation of one particular factory when similar factories would receive less favourable treatment simply because their employees were deemed to be less likely to commit crimes if their factories closed. Another example: screening for certain forms of cancer might be found to be of particular benefit only to women in poorer households. Yet the government would find it politically very difficult to deny such screening to *all* women. In a Social Policy Bond regime, bondholders would put maximisation of their return per unit outlay, which in this case would be maximisation of the health returns from cancer screening to the taxpayers' dollar, above such considerations.

Uniform approaches often go hand-in-hand with government's tendency to enlarge its own role. Government often applies its regulations regardless of whether or not they are appropriate in particular circumstances. Take the costs of complying with burdensome regulations for small businesses. The UK's Care Standards Act of 2000, is just one of many instances. It obliges every care home to have at least 14.1 square metres of private and public space for each elderly resident and at least eight single rooms for every double room. This sort of legislation has meant that over the past five years, at a time when the number of dependent elderly people in the UK has been rising, 50 000 care-home beds have been lost—about ten per cent of the total—and as a result 5000 much-needed hospital beds are occupied by elderly people who do not have acute medical needs.[8] Another example: potential employers can be deterred from starting a business because a government body insists that would-be employees are at risk from, for example, an absence of fire escapes. Government denies people the choice of whether to accept a slightly higher risk of a fatal accident at work, in return for a job. While it is all very well to protect workers in this way, when people cannot find work locally they have to travel. In doing so they may well face a risk of dying in a car accident far higher than that of being trapped in a building with no fire escapes. Other examples are even more obviously absurd. The European Union, for instance, insists that abattoirs be tiled. Logic therefore dictated that a snail farmer was told to tile his packing room, which was classed as an abattoir, up to the ceiling to catch the blood.[9]

Social Policy Bonds would encourage investigation of local circumstances, on the basis that doing so could lead to more efficient ways of achieving targeted outcomes than a uniform approach. The most efficient solutions for many social and environmental problems are *not* always known in advance, and the optimal choice is seldom a one-size fits all, top-down, government-dictated policy. More often, it is a matter for investigation and experimentation, and a wide variety of approaches is essential. Bondholders might find, after a bit of experimenting with different approaches, that certain activities work better than others under certain conditions. They would take the best of these approaches, and apply them where their return would be greatest, and they would recognise that, for certain objectives, a mosaic of diverse activities would be most efficient.

EFFICIENT COSTING OF OBJECTIVES

Many social and environmental objectives are difficult to value. Social Policy Bonds would share with conventional policy instruments the need for some estimate of the value to society of a specified objective. But they have an advantage over most other instruments in that the cost of achieving the targeted outcome would be minimised and capped. And if bondholders failed to perform, the budgetary cost to the taxpayer would be zero. In maximising the efficiency with which the outcome were achieved, the market for the bonds would be elegantly efficient in conveying information about the cost of achieving objectives and, crucially for policymakers, how this cost varies with time and circumstances.

Take, for example, the objective of lowering some index of water pollution from 50 to 40 units. Assume that the government issued one million bonds targeting water pollution, each redeemable for $10 once this lower level has been attained. The *maximum* cost to the government of achieving this objective would then be $10 million. But if the bonds, when issued, fetched $5 each, then the market would be saying that it thought it could achieve this objective for just $5 million. It wouldn't say *when* it thought it could achieve that objective, but that could be inferred from market behaviour and the market value of the bonds compared with other financial indicators. But what if the bonds sold for virtually nothing, and the market value of the bonds failed to move from that floor? That would mean that the government had miscalculated: in the market's view there would be no realistic chance of the objective being achieved for an outlay of $10 million in the foreseeable future. The government could respond in different ways:

- It could wait for new technology to arrive, or for circumstances to change in other ways, such that the market would see the objective as becoming more easily achievable, and the value of the bonds would consequently rise. Or

- It could issue more bonds, with the same specification, also redeemable for $10. It might do this in stages, gauging the market reaction to each new tranche of bonds, which would tell government the maximum cost of achieving the objective.

Either way, the government could be reasonably sure that it would be getting a good deal, expressed as 'reduction in water pollution per unit outlay'. This important benefit was mentioned in chapter 2, but is worth spelling out in more detail. Valuing the *benefit* of achieving an environmental outcome is bound to be an uncertain, and to some extent, subjective task, whichever policy instrument is used. But minimising the *cost* of whatever outcome is targeted is a different matter. A government issuing Social Policy Bonds could determine the maximum cost of achieving the objective because that would simply be the total number of bonds issued multiplied by the redemption value *plus* administration costs *minus* any revenues gained on floating the bonds. And, under a Social Policy Bond regime, it would be the collective wisdom of those in the market for bonds that would determine how much the government (that is, taxpayers) would actually pay to achieve the targeted outcome: they would have every incentive to minimise that cost.

But the bond mechanism would not merely minimise the *total* cost of achieving a specified objective. It would also indicate the *marginal* cost of achieving further improvements. Say the one million water pollution reduction bonds were to sell for $5 each. This would tell the government that the present value of the expected maximum cost, including bondholders' profits, of reducing water pollution from 50 to 40 units would be $5 million. The government might then suppose that it could afford to be more ambitious, and aim for a further fall in pollution to 30 units. It could issue a million additional bonds redeemable when this new lower concentration were reached. These would (probably) have an initial market value of less than $5, reflecting the (probably) diminishing returns involved in lowering the nitrate concentration. The point is that, by letting the market do the pricing of the bonds, the government would be getting an informed view of the *marginal* cost of its objectives. So if the bonds targeting the new level of 30 units were to sell for $4 each, then the maximum cost of achieving that objective would be $11 million, being equal to: $5 million (paid out when the level fell from 50 to 40 units) plus $6 million (paid out when the level fell from 40 to 30 units). The marginal cost of a 10-unit drop in water pollution would thus have been revealed to have risen from $5 million to $6 million. Should the government aim for a further fall to 20 units? Following such water pollution-targeting bond issues *it would have robust information about the cost of doing so.*

This is, of course, a simplified example and in fact the bond market would continuously update its pricing information. Say that improvements in technology, of the sort that might be stimulated by an initial water pollution targeting bond issue, made it much cheaper for farmers to reduce their water pollution emissions. Bondholders may, for example, have financed successful research into new varieties of grasses that exhibit better uptake of nitrogen fertiliser that would otherwise pollute rivers. How would the market react to such a development? Once the new varieties' effectiveness had been revealed, the value of all the bonds would rise. Instead of being priced at $5 and $4, the two water pollution issues of the example might sell for $8 and $7. The total cost to the government of redeeming these bonds would not change: it would remain at $11 million (though redemption would most probably occur earlier). But the market would be generating new information as to the likely cost of future improvements in water quality. The market would now be expecting reductions of 10 units of water pollution to cost $2 million (from 50 to 40 units), and $3 million (from 40 to 30 units). The new grass varieties would have reduced the costs from $5 million and $6 million (respectively). So the cost of any further pollution reductions would also fall, and by following market price movements policymakers could gauge approximately by how much.

These figures are hypothetical, but they do indicate the role that markets for Social Policy Bonds could play in helping the government, and taxpayers, decide on their spending priorities. The importance of this sort of market information can hardly be exaggerated. The failure in history of central planning can plausibly be attributed to the absence of market-generated information.[10] Market prices reflect all of the information used by all who transact, or choose not to transact, in the market. Central planning fails in comparison with a market economy because it encounters the limits of human beings' calculating capacity: no individual or group of individual planners knows or feasibly can know all the dispersed information that is embodied in prices. Even with a sound incentive system in place—and the centrally planned economies had some fearsome systems—without the information that only markets can generate the computational task of organising an efficient allocation of resources is too great. Prices incorporate and simplify all of the dispersed information implicit in getting a product or service to the marketplace. Markets for Social Policy Bonds would continually generate and reveal this information to policymakers and all those involved in achieving social and environmental outcomes—probably for the first time on a systematic basis. *A Social Policy*

Bond regime would combine market information with incentives to use it efficiently: the synergies arising could be of enormous benefit to society as a whole.

TRANSPARENCY

Social Policy Bonds would make policy objectives more *transparent*. By focusing on outcomes, rather than activities, they would explicitly identify social objectives. They would encourage indirect, as well as direct, means of achieving them: efficiency would be the overriding criterion. Focusing on identifiable outcomes would encourage constructive participation in the political process, and that would mean that measures taken to achieve them would be more likely to attract public support. At least as important, a bond regime would stipulate the maximum value that society wished to place on an outcome. This would have to be decided and made explicit before any bonds could be issued. Costing outcomes in this way would make the tradeoffs between social outcomes more transparent, and make more realistic people's expectations of government. In today's politics, costs of achieving outcomes are obscure, and the language of political debate, at least in the mass media, rarely includes the crucial concept of tradeoffs between different social goals.

Transparency in goal-setting would make virtually impossible two further obstacles on the way to efficient achievement of social goals:

- 'Capture' by bureaucrats: transparency of policy goals would make government unlikely to name itself the beneficiary of its own policies.

- Taxpayers' funding of corporate and middle-class welfare: bonds would make explicit the desired outcomes, and so would make it more difficult for government to launch projects that in effect tax the poor for the benefit of the middle class or the rich.

Transparency means clear and explicit objectives. Consider the European Union's Common Agricultural Policy. Its supposed objectives, as laid down in 1957 in the Treaty of Rome (1957), are:

1. to increase agricultural productivity,

2. to ensure a fair standard of living for [farmers], and

3. to assure the availability of [food] supplies,

4. ...at reasonable prices.[11]

These vague, mutually conflicting and open-ended objectives would not have been acceptable to people formulating desired outcomes for targeting by Social Policy Bonds. A bond regime would force a rethink on other policy issues. Drugs policy, for instance. Under a bond regime it would be difficult to avoid asking hard questions. Is a reduction in drug taking an end in itself, or a means to an end? If the latter, then what are these ends, and would it not be more efficient and transparent to target them directly? Unemployment may also have to be seen in a new light. Again, is lower unemployment an end in itself? Or a means to an end? Some studies have indeed suggested that the strongest influence on happiness is employment: people with jobs are very much happier than the unemployed.[12] But if lower unemployment were seen mainly as a way of ensuring that fewer people fall below a certain income level; or if it were seen as a means of lowering the crime rate, or improving mental health, then some combination of these objectives should be the targets for government policy. Answers to questions such as these would be unavoidable *at the outset* of a Social Policy Bond issue, but they are rarely posed, and still more rarely answered, under the existing policymaking regime.

Even where there is increased pressure for accountability under the existing regime, policies such at the Common Agricultural Policy have a momentum of their own. It is never made transparent, of course, but for those who administer these policies and their other beneficiaries, any visionary goals were largely forgotten along time ago, to be replaced by the goal of perpetuating the policies themselves and the institutions that administer them.

Transparent social goals would require a transparent process for formulating them. And a clear expression of desired social outcomes and their relative priorities would mean that progress toward them could be accurately monitored. Such transparency would also make the sources of any policy errors or deficiencies more identifiable. Perhaps that is one reason why it has rarely been a major feature of government activity over the decades.

MORE ATTRACTIVE MONEY FLOWS

A further advantage of Social Policy Bonds is that, in many cases, they would have more politically appealing money flows. Consider environmental policy. Most current methods of pollution control inflict identifiable losses on certain people in pursuit of vague objectives. Social Policy Bonds, however, would reward people for achieving successful outcomes. The bonds would of course be redeemed by funds from the issuing government's general taxation revenue, and taxes would still have to be levied to provide this but there is, nevertheless, a presentational advantage.

The other, more significant, money flow advantage of Social Policy Bonds is that the government would incur expenditure only when definite outcomes had actually been achieved. For this reason, the bonds may attract greater political support for certain causes than agency—or activity—based programmes.

CORRELATION WITH PUBLIC BENEFIT

A less obvious benefit of a Social Policy Bond regime would arise from the existence of a means of acquiring wealth whereby private gain would be strongly and inextricably correlated with public benefit. Many bondholders, whether institutions or individuals, would start out rich and, if their bonds rose in value, would become richer. But working successfully to achieve desired social goals would most likely be seen as a laudable way of acquiring wealth. There are intangible benefits from having people or institutions grow rich in this way. There are many disaffected people who, in some cases no doubt justifiably, view with suspicion or alarm the very high incomes or (apparent) profits of corporations engaged in activities of little obvious net social or environmental benefit. They are also unconvinced that 'trickledown' occurs to any meaningful degree. Wealth, in these people's eyes, is the result of exploitation. Social Policy Bonds would shift this worldview and, by helping people take a more positive view of the act of earning an income and accumulating wealth, could make for a more cohesive society.

STABILITY

A Social Policy Bond regime would help guarantee stability of policy objectives. Bonds could target goals with a necessarily long lead time and bondholders would not be deterred from taking measures to achieve them by fears of a reversal of government policy—or, indeed, a change of government. Only the ends of policies, not the means, would be laid down by government. Obviously the objectives would have to be carefully defined, but there is a wide consensus over what constitutes most social goals. A government would be unlikely to repudiate such universally desired *objectives*, even if a ruling party with a different political outlook had issued the associated Social Policy Bonds. The risk that it might (and so become the first government *openly* to support higher unemployment, lower standards of health care, etc) would be not much greater than that of a government refusing to redeem fixed interest stock issued by any of its predecessors. This risk, always present, is factored into the prices of conventional government-issued bonds, and in no way impedes the operation of bond markets.

Importantly, governments would have to give assurances as to their future behaviour if the bonds were to be as successful as possible. For maximum success, they would also have to choose their objectives in consultation with opposition political parties as well as the electorate.

Because Social Policy Bonds could target broad objectives, which are more likely to be stable over time, they would probably have *informational advantages* over more narrowly specified policies. As an example, let us take the myriad ways in which health care funding can be allocated. The government has to make these resource allocation decisions on the basis of data that are necessarily incomplete. How can the government know in detail the effect that spending on, say, cancer diagnostic machinery will have on the overall health of the nation, as compared with subsidising the cost of nicotine chewing gum? So, by default, health expenditure is influenced by groups of medical specialists with little incentive or capacity to see improvements in the *general* health of the nation as an objective. As a result, funding of these specialities depends to a great and varying extent, on the strength of their lobby groups or on their public profile, rather than on what would best meet the needs of society. Consider the British national health care system's terminal-care budget: 95 per cent of this is allocated to the 25 per cent of the UK's population who die from cancer, and just 5 per cent to the 75 per cent who die from all other causes.[13]

Stable objectives would also mean that rational allocation of resources would not be undermined by high-profile events. For instance, in the aftermath of a tragic rail disaster in London that resulted in the deaths of 40 people the UK Government came under considerable pressure to order the installation of an automatic braking system for trains that go through red signals. Cold calculations showed that this would cost around $21 million for each life that the system could be expected to save. This is around five times the figure that the UK Treasury used as its benchmark valuation of a human life, which means that if the government had succumbed to pressure to install the automatic braking system it would have diverted funds from more cost-effective life-saving projects, and so caused the loss of more lives than it would have saved. A Social Policy Bond regime that had as its objective the maximising of the number of lives saved per government dollar would not waver in the face of one-off events.

Stable objectives would also mean that uncertain scientific relationships need not be proven beyond doubt before work could begin on achieving them. This advantage, and the other advantages that come from long-term stability of policy goals, combine to make the bonds a better policy for some large-scale environmental problems, of which climate change is one.

EXAMPLE 1: CLIMATE STABILITY BONDS

The evidence that the global climate is changing is large and growing. That said, scientists are divided as to (a) how fast climate is changing, (b) the effects of climate change (c) how much people can do about it, and (d) how much people should do about it. And there are still respectable scientists who argue that the climate is not changing at all in any meaningful way. Despite these uncertainties, climate change has the potential to inflict serious harm on many people, so there is a strong argument for doing what is necessary to minimise its adverse effects.

The December 1997 Kyoto Protocol ('Kyoto') saw 159 nations reach the world's first legally binding commitments to reduce the global output of carbon dioxide and five other gases thought to contribute to the 'greenhouse' effect. Thirty-eight industrialised countries agreed to reduce emissions by 2012 to an average of 5.2 per cent below their 1990 levels and, in July 2001, 180 countries reached a broad political agreement on the operational rules that will govern the Protocol.

The Kyoto targets are far lower than those that some environmentalists had hoped for, and that some countries, most notably the European Union, had been advocating. Kyoto will only slow, but not stop, the build-up of carbon dioxide and other greenhouse gases in the atmosphere. (Carbon dioxide, which is given off by fossil fuel combustion, is thought to be by far the most important of the man-made greenhouse gases that form an insulating blanket around Earth.) But subsequent evaluations by leading scientists indicate that the environmental effects may be so small as to be almost unnoticeable in the near term.

CLIMATE STABILITY BONDS

Kyoto embodies the assumption that controlling the targeted greenhouse gases is the best way of achieving climate stability. But with climate change, the biological and physical relationships involved are many and complex. Even specialists disagree about the degree to which the multitude of biological and physical variables influences climate change. Apart from the daunting uncertainties about the role of greenhouse gases in climate change, there is even less understanding of the role that agriculture and forestry can play as sinks for these gases.

A bond regime targeting climate stability would bypass these, and other, uncertainties, and encourage research into clarifying the relevant scientific relationships. Climate Stability Bonds would be issued on the open market and would become redeemable for a fixed sum only when the climate had reached an agreed and sustained level of stability.[14] In this way there would be no need for the targeting mechanism to make assumptions as to *how* to stabilise the world climate: that would be left to bondholders.

Ideally Climate Stability Bonds would be internationally backed. They could be issued by a world body, possibly one supervised by the United Nations or World Bank. This body would undertake to redeem the bonds using funds that could perhaps be obtained from all countries, in proportion to their Gross Domestic Product. It would be up to individual countries to decide how to raise funds—presumably they would do so from taxation revenue. Importantly though, no bonds would be redeemed until the objective of a more stable climate has been achieved and sustained. Climate Stability Bonds would be issued by open tender, as at an auction; those who bid the highest price for the limited number of bonds would be successful in buying them. A fixed number of bonds would be issued redeemable for, say, $1 million each, only when climate stability, as certified by objective measurements made by independent scientific bodies, had been achieved and sustained. As with all other Social Policy Bonds, once issued, Climate Stability Bonds would be freely tradable on the open market.

People would differ in their valuation of the bonds, and their views would change as events occurred that made achievement of a stable climate a more or less remote prospect. They would also change when new information about climate, and about the causes of climate change, was discovered.

There are obvious difficulties involved in defining what a stable climate actually is, *but the same difficulties apply when attempting to monitor the success or otherwise of Kyoto.* Presumably scientists will monitor such objectively verifiable indicators as temperature, change in temperature, rate of change of temperature, precipitation, and many others, at a wide range of locations.

Climate Stability Bonds would be redeemed only when climate stability, as defined by such a set of indicators, had been achieved. A bond regime would also have the flexibility explicitly to target less scientific measures, such as the frequency and severity of adverse climatic events, the numbers of people killed or made homeless by such events, or the insurance payouts to which they give rise.

WHAT MIGHT BONDHOLDERS DO?

A Climate Stability Bond regime would not dictate how to achieve a stable climate. Bondholders could undertake a wide range of projects including:

- helping countries or companies to set up and run greenhouse gas emission control programmes;

- helping countries or companies to set up carbon sequestration plantations;

- investigating innovative ways of removing greenhouse gases from the atmosphere; or

- carrying out, or supporting, research into increasing the reflectiveness of the Earth or its atmosphere.

Bondholders could also be expected to finance other research and initiatives, all aimed at stabilising climate as cost-effectively as possible.

Some governments, research institutes and others are already carrying out these or similar activities. But, under a Climate Stability Bond regime, bondholders would have an incentive to seek out those ways of achieving a stable climate that would give them the best return on what is, in effect, the taxpayers' outlay. Only when the targeted degree of climate stability were achieved would governments have to pay for it by redeeming the bonds. Until then, bondholders would have to finance the initiatives that they think would achieve climate stability. The body that issues the bonds would, in effect, contract out the achievement of climate stability to the private sector—having defined the nature and degree of the stability that it wanted, and undertaken to pay bondholders once it had been achieved.

ADVANTAGES OF CLIMATE STABILITY BONDS

Climate Stability Bonds would have two critical advantages over Kyoto. One is that they would encourage people to do whatever is necessary to achieve climate stability. The bonds would not rely on the robustness of our existing scientific knowledge even as to whether the climate is changing in the way that many scientists believe it is, let alone as to how best to stabilise it. Kyoto aims to reduce emissions of a small range of gases. But there may be other causes of climate change that are far more important, of which we are currently unaware. And these need not be man-made: natural variability of climate has had severe impacts on human life in the past[15] and could still be playing a role. Kyoto, responding to effects whose causes are uncertain, embodies a limited number of fixed ideas about the nature of the relationships involved. A bond regime targeting climate change directly might well lead to cuts in greenhouse gas emissions, *but it would not assume that doing so is the best solution.* Climate Stability Bonds would improve on Kyoto because they would encourage behaviour leading to the desired outcome, rather than seek to control activities whose effects on climate stability are not fully known.

The other major advantage of a bond regime is that bondholders would be motivated to be efficient in achieving climate stability. They would initiate whichever climate-stabilising projects they thought would give them the best return for their outlay. The more efficient bondholders were in achieving climate stability the more they would gain from appreciation of the value of their bonds. Their efficiency would maximise the degree of climate stability that *society as a whole* would achieve per dollar outlay. Because of the colossal sums involved, the benefits that Climate Stability Bonds could offer in comparison with activity-based regimes, such as Kyoto, could be huge.

Further advantages of a bond regime would be:

- That funds for climate stability would not need to be used for scien tifically approved projects. They could, for instance, be used to bribe corrupt or malicious governments. Appealing to these governments' financial self-interest could be the most effective way of modifying their behaviour in favour of achieving climate stability.

- That governments would pay up only when a stable climate had been achieved: any risk of failure or of undershooting the climate stability target would be borne by bondholders, rather than taxpayers.

- That formulating the redemption terms for Climate Stability Bonds would entail clarifying of what is actually wanted. In global terms, climate change—as distinct from climate variability—could actually be a good thing. It could lead to longer growing seasons and higher yields in some regions, or boost crop productivity because higher levels of atmospheric carbon dioxide can act as a fertiliser.[16] 'Climate stability' as targeted by Climate Stability Bonds could be defined such that bondholders would tackle only the negative effects of climate change.

Following up this last point, there might be large immediate benefits for humanity if one component of the goal targeted by Climate Stability Bonds were 'the numbers killed or made homeless by adverse climatic conditions'. A bond regime would allow that sort of flexibility; Kyoto does not.

Trying to stabilise the world's climate, whichever way is chosen, is going to require a huge range of different projects. Reducing greenhouse gas emissions or sequestering carbon might be helpful, but they are not necessarily going to be cost-effective. Other ways yet to be discovered could be far cheaper. Kyoto is deficient in that it offers no incentives to find out how to achieve a stable climate most cost-effectively. Climate Stability Bonds would encourage the most efficient solutions given the knowledge available at any time, and they would stimulate research into finding ever more cost-effective solutions. This would occur because of the nature of the bond mechanism, and would require no presupposition as to the optimal set of solutions. The bond issuers would dictate only the objective—climate stability—not the ways of achieving it. Crucially too, this objective could be so defined as to attract more political and public support than Kyoto's cuts in greenhouse gas emissions. Without such support no policy addressing climate change is likely to be coherent, let alone successful.

5

Comparison with other 'more-market' approaches

Many countries' governments have recognised the inadequacies of the conventional approach to solving social problems. Recognising that the market is better at allocating scarce resources than government, they have made various efforts to give the market more influence over these decisions. This chapter looks at some of these alternatives, and contrasts them with Social Policy Bonds.

TRADABLE PERMITS TO POLLUTE

A tradable permit regime determines the maximum amount of pollutant that can be discharged. People then trade permits to emit amounts of pollutant making up this total. Markets decide the price and allocation of the permits. Tradable permits are most relevant to unpriced resources, such as the assimilative capacity of the environment. They are most widely used in pollution control and are best applied to limit emissions of pollutants that have marked thresholds. In the US, markets for permits to emit sulphur dioxide have been in operation for several years.

As we saw in the previous chapter, a Social Policy Bond regime could have informational advantages when targeting broad objectives. These advantages could be significant when there are large numbers of polluters, or where scientific relationships are uncertain.

However, tradable permits can work well with intrinsically large-scale processes, or for controlling emissions that have no polluting substitutes. Such processes and substances can be monitored and controlled quite easily, because doing so is unlikely to lead to offsetting increases in pollution via the setting up of difficult-to-monitor small-scale processes, or the emission of polluting substitutes that are not being monitored. But technological and ecological complexities mean that these processes and substances are a minority. Water pollution, for example, results from many sources and many different processes. Immense quantities of information would be needed to establish, monitor and enforce a comprehensive system of pollution control using tradable permits to pollute. A bond regime, however, could be more flexible. It could target an index of 'water pollution', embodying many pollutants, whose weights in the index would differ according to their adverse effects on the environment. In general, it is air or water pollution as a whole, or the adverse effects of such pollution, that need control, not the concentrations of single pollutants.

It seems likely that tradable permits to pollute will continue to play only a small role in environmental protection.

PRIVATISATION

Privatisation is the selling of assets owned by government suppliers of services and the transfer of control to shareholders. It has been widespread. In many countries utilities, such as railways, electricity companies and telecoms have been fully privatised. In the UK most of the local authorities' housing stock has been sold to ex-tenants.

How successful has privatisation been? In those countries with rule of law and secure property rights it has had some success, at least when compared to the performance of nationalised industries. There have been some improvements in efficiency, and because of the taxes they pay on their profits, privatised companies now make positive contributions to government funds—a dramatic change from when they were publicly owned and were mostly a drain on public funds. But some of the labour the industries shed on privatisation has not found alternative employment, and it appears that it was government's disengagement from day-to-day operating decisions, rather than the transfer of ownership, that secured privatisation's efficiency gains.[17] Customers have on balance gained from privatisation, but not hugely. There have been significant improvements in service to customers where businesses have faced competition, as in telecoms and airlines. Fears that privatisation would lead to a loss of universal service or to higher charges for the poor have proved unfounded,[18] but again, regulatory policy has probably been an important factor. Privatisation, according to another view, has apparently created a need for very detailed public regulation of privatised industries, and this has been quite at odds with what was expected by the government and its advisors. What we have now 'is not a clear case of the state withdrawing as an economic agent but rather changing its role as such.'[19] This might be one reason why, despite widespread privatisation, the volume of government spending has hardly fallen in the industrialised countries.

Privatisation of services like basic education, health care, and social insurance would probably not be politically acceptable in many countries; at least, not without further extensive regulation. The problem is that private businesses have private goals, and while these may coincide with social goals some or even most of the time, there will always be some people who either through their own, or their parents', misfortune, indolence or apathy, will not be well-served by private institutions pursuing purely private goals. This, of course, is true of the current system, but the current system can claim that because it is not private it has the public interest at heart. (It may be failing to look after the public interest, and it may be very expensive and inefficient, but it can make that claim.) A fully privatised school system, for instance, would have no market incentive to raise the educational standards of the less bright children of poor parents.

In short, privatisation can be helpful as one way of giving more meaningful incentives for people to run services currently run by government agents. But private companies are not generally rewarded for achieving desirable social outcomes. Privatisation is merely a transfer of assets, or a disengagement of government from the running of certain activities. By itself, it cannot supplant the government's role as a safety net for the neediest members of society or as a provider of public goods.

VOUCHER SCHEMES

Education voucher schemes have been used by several states in the northeastern US, and in the UK. Parents are given vouchers that they can use to purchase schooling for their children from whichever schools they wish, whether they be government or private.

Vouchers assign greater importance to the demands that consumers actually make of an education system, rather than to the services that government employees or others think they should want. Most parents agree on the importance of basic academic subjects. They expect that, at a minimum, their children will have mastered reading, writing, and elementary maths by the time they are out primary school. Parents are also concerned about career preparation. But beyond these basics, priorities differ widely. Vouchers allow parents to make their own decisions, and encourage schools to compete to supply what parents want.

Voucher schemes have some of the advantages of Social Policy Bonds: through markets parents are motivated to seek the best education available at the price, and schools are motivated to supply it. Under a voucher scheme government continues to pay for education. But vouchers do have some disadvantages. Some of these stem from the fact that the vouchers do not specify outcomes. They specify only that they must be used to pay for children's going to school. This works well for those children whose parents are capable of making informed choices, and who are willing to do so. It does not work so well for the children of less informed or less motivated parents, and these are precisely those who most need help. So under a voucher system, it would still be possible for desired social outcomes, such as universal literacy, say, not to be achieved. Another concern is that vouchers could encourage the negative aspects of competitive behaviour. Under a Social Policy Bond regime rewards from self-interest would be inextricably tied to outcomes. In voucher schemes, on the other hand, self-interest could take the form of suppliers competing against each other in ways that undermine their ability to achieve targeted outcomes efficiently. This is especially likely when consumers lack information, as is likely to be the case in, say, provision of health services.

As well, voucher systems could not readily be applied to goals that have a strong public good element such as better law and order, improved health care, and better environmental protection. These concerns would make it difficult to apply voucher schemes widely.

CONTRACTUAL APPROACH: NEW ZEALAND STATE SECTOR REFORM

Over several years beginning in 1988, New Zealand's public sector was radically and innovatively reformed. Tightly held central control gave way to autonomous departments, headed by chief executives with the authority to take decisions relating to the whole of their organisations. Chief executives are now expected to hire and fire staff, negotiate pay, manage their finances and capital assets, negotiate purchase agreements and be held to account for outputs. Other relevant features of the New Zealand public sector are that:

- accountability for resources and results is maintained through contestable, contract-like arrangements within government;

- performance agreements between government ministers and chief executives lay down standards and expectations for department heads; and

- purchase agreements between ministers and departments specify the outputs to be produced during the year.

The arrangements between ministers and departments specify *ex ante* the outputs they are required to deliver, but leave chief executives free to select the mix of inputs to be used in producing these outputs (see box, *Essential terms*). This system has been extended to encompass the specification of, and accountability for, longer-term objectives. Since 1994 the New Zealand Government has defined the medium-term outcomes it is trying to achieve in nine 'strategic result areas' (SRAs) and linked the outputs delivered by each department to these SRAs through 'key result areas', which form the basis of their performance agreements.

Essential terms

Inputs Expenditure, or those factors of production, such as staff, accommodation, other supplies, or other resources, that are used to produce goods and services. Amongst the inputs devoted to lowering crime, for example, would be: police numbers; numbers of patrol cars; and expenditure on policing.

Outputs Products that are directly attributable to the performance of an agency, such as number of reports produced and distributed or number of buildings constructed. Outputs of a crime-fighting agency could be: numbers of police on the beat or on patrol at a time; number of police stations open 24 hours a day; number of toll-free phone lines; proportion of police emergency phone calls answered within 15 seconds.

Outcomes, objectives, goals Desirable sets of circumstances, which are likely to be influenced by both an agent's outputs, and by factors outside agents' control. Outcomes that might be targeted by crime-fighting agencies include: a crime rate 10 per cent lower than in the previous year (as measured by number of reported crimes, or responses to victim surveys). The terms 'objectives' and 'goals' are used synonymously in this text to mean desired outcomes.

Indicators Quantifiable measures that can be used singly or in combination to chart progress towards objectives.

What have the results been? According to a report commissioned by the New Zealand Government, there have been efficiency gains. However, the transactions costs incurred in negotiating agreements, monitoring compliance and preparing reports have been high, and in many cases have 'soaked up a substantial part of the efficiency gains' made from restructuring.[20]

In the context of bureaucratic change the New Zealand reforms were radical. But the reforms were constrained by the then existing institutional structures. At the outset of the reform programme, government departments had been envisaged as achieving specific *outcomes*. But that vision did not carry through. Instead, outputs became the measure by which departments' performance is judged; the rationale being that the supply of outputs can be directly attributed to departments' performance, while outcomes can be influenced by factors beyond their control. As Schick puts it: 'outcomes are externalities in two-party relationships; therefore it is exceedingly difficult to assign responsibility for them.' The need to assign responsibility arises only because the players—those charged with doing things—are largely known in advance. They are the existing government departments, of course. A cynic might say that, in effect, the New Zealand reforms have subordinated results to what appears to be the overriding need to assign responsibility, which in turn, seems to be driven by existing institutional structures and relationships.

CONTRACTING OUT OF EXISTING SERVICES AND THE UK'S PRIVATE FINANCE INITIATIVE

Chapter 2 briefly looked at some of the limitations involved in handing responsibility for services to private contractors. When compared to Social Policy Bonds, contracting out has other disadvantages. Take the UK Government's Private Finance Initiative (PFI), which aims to encourage the private sector to invest in major public infrastructure projects, such as hospitals, schools, and roads. Under the PFI, building projects that would previously have relied on public money are financed by the private sector. Government specifies the outputs it requires, in terms of the nature and level of service required, and invites the private sector to bid for the contract to supply these outputs. Taking hospitals, for example, the private sector partner is usually responsible for:

- designing the facilities according to National Health Service (NHS) specifications;

- building the facilities to time and at a fixed cost;

- financing the capital cost: the private sector partner recovers this cost by renting the facilities to the NHS, generally for periods of more than 25 years; and

- operating the facilities: most of the staff, including cleaners, catering, porters, security and maintenance staff, are employed by the private contractor. Receptionists, secretaries and lab technicians may also be employed by the private sector (but doctors and nurses are employed by the NHS).

When using the PFI the UK Government is, in effect, contracting out the building of the hospital and non-health staffing to the private sector. It is the private sector PFI partner that assumes the risks in each of these areas; this reduces the overall risks to the public sector associated with procuring new assets. Moreover, because the PFI partner's capital is at risk, it will have a strong incentive to continue to perform efficiently throughout the life of the contract.

The PFI, as with contracting out of services generally, is efficient at supplying carefully specified outputs. Specification of these outputs can be a costly exercise (though costs will fall as different public sector bodies share their output-specification experiences), as is the monitoring of compliance, but allowing the private sector to bid to supply outputs is generally more efficient than paying directly from public funds. A report commissioned by the UK Treasury puts the average estimated saving for a sample of projects as 17 per cent.[21] Nevertheless, because it is only outputs that are specified under the PFI, and because of the degree to which they must be specified to ensure efficiency, the PFI, as with contracting out of services generally tends:

- to be limited to particular stages of an outcome-delivering enterprise; and

- to reinforce established ways of doing things.

Outputs, however efficiently supplied, do not necessarily lead to more favourable, or more efficiently supplied, outcomes. So under the PFI a new hospital may be more likely to be built on time, to exact specification, and cost-effectively. But a Social Policy Bond targeting general health indicators would not assume that a new hospital were the best way of achieving society's health goals in the first place.

TRADABLE CONTRACTS

What if public sector contracts were made tradable, so that the winner of a tendered contract could sell the right to supply the service? Perhaps the successful bidding company would have done what it could to achieve a targeted objective, and done so efficiently and quickly. So the value of the contract would have risen, and being tradable, could be sold at a profit. The new contractor would then still have an incentive to perform efficiently. Tradable contracts would be similar to Social Policy Bonds, as long as the terms of the contract stipulated that a specified outcome be achieved, rather than an output be supplied. A contract's tradability would help avoid the problem of possible collusion (tacit or not) between bidders for contracts; under the current system, inflated bids can succeed if the bidders agree (explicitly or not) to inflate their bids.

Tradability of contracts would encourage suppliers of services to continue to minimise costs and maintain efficiency *after* they have started helping achieve the targeted goal. Under the current system there may be a tendency for contractors, or their employees, having won a contract, not to maximise the speed and efficiency with which they go about solving the targeted problem or, more likely, supplying the agreed output. While contractors can sometimes benefit from being efficient, they cannot always enjoy this benefit in terms of immediate cash capital gains. There is scope for incentive payments, or penalty clauses, but these are crude, ad hoc arrangements that are costly to administer or impose. Under a Social Policy Bond regime, if bondholders were unexpectedly efficient (or if external events were unexpectedly helpful) they could sell their bonds and realise their capital gains before all the necessary work had been carried out. And if bondholders were inefficient, *they* would be the losers, not taxpayers. The same benefit, in principle, would apply to tradable contracts to achieve an outcome.

Tradability would also transfer the risk of breach of contract from the tax—or rate—payer to bondholders. If, under a contract system, the successful bidders fail to do what they were legally obliged to do, then it is up to the aggrieved party—the central or local government agency—to take proceedings against them. Even if such actions are successful, they can be protracted and costly. Under a tradable contract or Social Policy Bond regime, underperforming investors would find a ready market for their contract or bonds in people who believe they can be more efficient.

The main difference between a tradable contract to deliver an outcome, and a Social Policy Bond issue, would be that Social Policy Bonds could be bought and held by anybody, not just people already involved in carrying out the target-achieving projects, or well set up to do so. So the number of possible bidders would not be limited to a few likely operators, but would be open to all who are prepared to do, or to finance the doing of, things that would help achieve the targeted objective. The fact that anybody could be involved in the bidding for bonds at any stage would discourage people from making excessive bids, so ensuring that social objectives would be achieved as cost-effectively as possible. Compared with tradable contracts, this would make ownership of Social Policy Bonds more fluid, which would mean more market liquidity, more transparency and an enhanced ability for the government to fine tune its priorities after the outcome has been specified and the bonds issued.

If the Social Policy Bond concept were to generate more market activity, it would make more practical the targeting of remote objectives; ones that may take years or decades to achieve. Many businesses would be reluctant to take on these goals without the possibility that they could benefit in the shorter run. Social Policy Bonds would allow them to do what they could to achieve the target, then benefit from selling their bonds at a higher price, letting the new bondholders continue the advance toward the goal. Similarly, a liquid market for the bonds would make it more quickly apparent that those charged with achieving a social goal had underestimated their costs, or overestimated their efficiency. Under a regime of tradable contracts for which there were no liquid market, such deficiencies might take a fatally long time to become obvious. But under a Social Policy Bond regime the market prices of the relevant bonds would fall, making it clear to everyone that the current contractors were inefficient, and making it easier for other investors to take hold of the reins and pursue the targeted objective. And, as we saw in chapter 4, there are other advantages arising from the information that the bonds' market prices would generate. To recap: markets in the bonds would continuously reveal information that would tell the issuers, and anyone who might want to supply objective-achieving services: (1) how close a targeted objective were to being achieved; (2) the potential rewards from buying the bonds and participating in objective-achieving projects; and (3) the likely costs of marginal improvements beyond those already targeted.

SUMMARY: SOCIAL POLICY BONDS COMPARED WITH OTHER 'MORE MARKET' APPROACHES

Both the *contractual arrangements* between government ministers and government agencies seen in the New Zealand state sector reforms, and the *contracting out* of existing services, suffer because of the need for government to specify in detail what is required. This limits their application considerably and adds to their implementation costs. Similarly, the information demands of tradable pollution permits mean that they can be used only for inherently large-scale processes that can be monitored quite easily.

One aspect of the UK's Private Finance Initiative that is particularly noteworthy has the private sector's willingness to bear the risks of overruns on such items as construction cost. Indeed, this transfer of risk to the private sector is estimated to account for 60 per cent of the forecast savings that result from the PFI.[22] The private sector's willingness to bear risk, and the savings that result, would bode well for a Social Policy Bond regime, under which investors in the bonds would bear all the risks of achieving outcomes. Because the market would determine the bonds' prices, the cost of assuming all risks would be fair to both bondholders as well as the taxpayer.

Because of the limitations inherent in the contracting out of services, it would seem that *privatisation* and *vouchers* are the most widely applicable of the 'more market' alternatives to government. A combination of privatised schools, for example, and vouchers, could do much to raise standards in education with unchanged, or even reduced, public expenditure. But note the problem of children whose parents have no ability to make an informed decision as to the schooling, or who have no interest in doing so. For education, this could turn out to be a minor problem—at least as compared with that generated by state systems—as the standards of all schools be probably rise in a privatised system. But lack of information would be marked in health care, where most consumers have little idea as to the treatment they need. They rely on the medical profession to tell them.

In general, when a system allows private interests to flourish, there will be some people who suffer either because they are poor, or because they are uninformed consumers. Giving the poor purchasing power would help them, but only insofar as they could make an informed decision, and would be willing to do so. When the service is one like education, most people would probably fall into that category. But when the service is one like health care, where most consumers are in the dark, the number of uninformed or misinformed people would be very large.

Social Policy Bonds would solve this information problem in ways that privatisation or voucher schemes, or combinations of the two, cannot. They would give a voice to, and focus directly on, *society's* concerns, expressed in terms of explicit desired outcomes. Compared to privatisation or voucher schemes, they would have advantages in education where some people's children may fall through the cracks, and they would have more significant advantages in health care, where most people are uninformed. There are important public good aspects in having an educated and healthy population. But where Social Policy Bonds would score heavily over other more-market mechanisms would be in the delivery of those objectives that have an even purer public character, such as reduced crime rates or a cleaner environment.

For the same reasons, they might also have political advantages. Most of the arguments in favour of continued government intervention in areas like health, education, and welfare crystallise around what would happen to the poor or unfortunate if government were to withdraw. Social Policy Bonds may be superior to other 'more market' approaches, in that government would not relinquish its role in bringing about better outcomes for the poorest members of society. It would simply withdraw from *achieving* these goals, but continue to set these goals, and to be the ultimate source of finance for their achievement. Society's goals are not the same as an aggregation of all its members' individual goals weighted by purchasing power. As a society, there are outcomes like safer neighbourhoods, lower infant mortality, or 100 per cent literacy, which people collectively might want to achieve, and know they can achieve, but which a fully privatised system would not guarantee. Social Policy Bonds, because of their focus on outcomes, would allow full discussion and consultation as to what society's goals are, and how much society values their achievement. They would then reward people for achieving them at least cost to society.

6

Social Policy Bonds, policy and politics

This chapter discusses looks first at likely sources of support and opposition to a bond regime. It then looks at how Social Policy Bonds would interact with and reshape the current policymaking environment. It goes on to look at how the bonds could be used in developing countries and concludes by outlining the case for Literacy Bonds, aimed at raising literacy in developing countries, as a more efficient and humane alternative to a 'war on terrorism'.

SUPPORT AND OPPOSITION

Much of the debate about government spending in the developed countries centres on its size, rather than its efficiency. Yet the two are linked: it is hard to voice the case for reducing the size of government when many social and environmental problems persist. It is arguable that they persist because the government programmes that are supposed to solve them actually reward activities, rather than solutions. People are paid for their time, rather than their success or efficiency. Typically, government programmes appear to be cumbersome and inefficient. They are often unresponsive to events and lack the ability to adapt to local circumstances.

Social Policy Bonds, on the other hand, would be explicitly focused on outcomes. As such, they might command wider political support than activity-based programmes. And because they would inject incentives into all stages necessary for solving social problems they would probably be more efficient than current efforts. Nevertheless, they might face opposition.

There would most probably be opposition from the public sector: those who currently face very limited competition in supplying services that would be made contestable under a Social Policy Bond regime. Public sector trade unions could be expected to resist Social Policy Bonds, in the same way as they have opposed privatisation, the UK's Private Finance Initiative or voucher schemes.

Other opponents could be those who believe they benefit from the current array of transfers and subsidies. There are many in industry and agriculture who benefit from perverse subsidies, as we saw in chapter 1, and who would suffer from the removal of their special privileges, at least in the short term. Many of these privileges are granted only because the identity of the people who receive them, and their true costs to everyone else, are not widely known. Opposition to a bond regime might also come from those who would be surprised to learn that they are net beneficiaries of lavish taxpayer subsidies, or barriers to imports, that often deliver more to the better off than to the poor and disadvantaged. Car drivers and rail passengers, for example, could find that they would lose out under a Social Policy Bond regime, whose focus on outcomes would oblige policymakers to identify more clearly exactly what or who would be the intended beneficiary of government spending.

It is also likely that there would be opposition from civil servants and others who administer transfer and subsidy programmes. Many of these people's jobs would probably gradually disappear during the transition to a Social Policy Bond regime, but of course there would be more, and more fulfilling jobs, created in a Social Policy Bond environment. Politicians might also oppose Social Policy Bonds, despite the likelihood that the bonds would achieve their stated objectives more readily. This opposition would come from a natural desire to hold on to power, including the policy instruments that a Social Policy Bond regime would transfer to the private sector.

However, support for Social Policy Bonds should come from those who are sincere in their wish to see improvements in the position of the poorest members of society and in the provision of public goods—and many politicians do fall into this category. These people would concentrate their energies on promoting the use of Social Policy Bonds that target the well-being of their constituents. More support for Social Policy Bonds would come from who already have some experience of contracting for the public sector. In general, the poor, and those who claim to represent them would support the bonds—if they were open-minded, and after experimental trials of the bonds had been shown to work. A more diffuse of support would be taxpayers, especially if trials of the bond concept had been successful, and once they saw either that targeted outcomes could be achieved at less cost to themselves or that they would not have to pay anything in the event of failure to achieve such outcomes.

EFFICIENCY AND TRANSPARENCY: A POTENT COMBINATION

Social Policy Bonds would combine efficiency in achieving social goals with transparency about exactly what these goals would be and how much they would cost to achieve. This combination of efficiency and transparency could generate its own dynamic and transform policy-making. It could take way much of government's discretion as to which interest groups receive this or that amount of public spending. The thrust of political debate would shift away from discussion about policy instruments and away from declarations of increased agency-based spending as though that were a sufficient measure of a government's contribution to achieving social goals. Instead the entire political process could shift towards:

- more consultation with voters as to what society's goals should be;

- seeking and articulating information as to the trade-offs that are involved in achieving particular social goals;

- defining society's goals in terms that people can understand and that are measurable; these goals would be explicit and would appear on election manifestos: their relative priority would be a matter for open political debate; and

- organising appropriate issues of Social Policy Bonds, and redeeming them once targeted social and environmental outcomes had been achieved.

Initially at least there would be some public services, such as defence, whose outcomes are difficult to define and quantify. And government would still have some discretionary powers to allocate finance to meet unexpected events, such as civil defence emergencies. But outcome-based policy, such as would be characteristic of a Social Policy Bond regime, would remove much of its discretionary power over how it spends its revenues.

There would be some benefits, however, to those in government. They would benefit to the extent that people would not automatically blame them if goals were not achieved. And because Social Policy Bonds would specify explicit outcomes and channel market forces into achieving them efficiently, government could concentrate more on identifying existing or new policy issues that have been neglected.

SIZE OF GOVERNMENT

What would any efficiency gains arising from a Social Policy Bond regime mean for the size of government? A government issuing Social Policy Bonds could most likely pursue its existing goals and achieve them more cheaply, and so lower the taxes it imposes on its citizens.

There would be many benefits from a smaller, more efficient government that solved social and environmental problems by issuing Social Policy Bonds. Apart from doing a better job of looking after the poorest members of society directly, smaller government, and a reduced tax burden would have further benefits.

1. Lower taxes reduce the burden to the economy by more than the taxes themselves. This is only partly because of savings in the administration costs that taxes impose. More important are the so-called deadweight costs of taxes. These arise because of the way taxes distort production and consumption behaviour. They mean that even if all tax revenue were handed straight back to producers and consumers, the economy as a whole would be worse off than if there were no taxes. Deadweight losses would be much reduced in a lower-tax environment.

2. Tax cuts have acquired something of a bad name in recent years, as the major beneficiaries of income tax cuts have probably been the rich. But it is important to realise that under a bond regime the poor would benefit not only from more efficient provision of services currently supplied by government, but also from future tax cuts. Many low-income earners face proportionately high marginal tax rates paying, as they do, both income taxes and social security taxes. Their employers are also likely to be paying a payroll tax. While a general cut in taxes would benefit the already wealthy, the poor would also gain significantly.

3. Many people object to big government not only on the grounds that it is inefficient, incompetent or worse, but also on the grounds that it infringes the liberty of its citizens, by virtue of size alone. For these people, smaller government would be an end in itself.

But there might well be a countervailing influence in the other direction. Because government would be more efficient and its goals more transparent and subject to consensus, people might well be willing to allow it a *larger* role. New environmental concerns are bound to present themselves, and the outcome-orientation of Social Policy Bonds could make government less wary about stipulating goals too in other areas, such as crime, where there is consensus over what result is required, but little agreement on how to get there.

In short, Social Policy Bonds would be compatible with smaller or larger government. Their prime focus would be on efficiency in achieving social and environmental outcomes. A government that used Social Policy Bonds as a major policy instrument might assume a smaller or larger role as a result. Either way it would be doing so in response to its citizens' wishes.

SOCIAL POLICY BONDS AND DEVELOPING COUNTRIES

So far this discussion has centred on developed countries. This has mostly been because the size of the public sector in developed countries is bigger than in the developing countries, and also because these countries' government policies and their performance are better documented. But Social Policy Bonds would in many ways be at least as well suited to application in developing countries. There are several reasons for this:

- Public sectors are growing even faster in developing countries than in the developed world from, of course, a smaller base. There is the opportunity therefore to avoid the mistakes that developed countries made when their public sectors grew.

- While public sectors in the developing countries are growing rapidly, they are still not big enough to cope with their very severe social problems and the enormous social changes that are occurring. Developing countries are urbanising rapidly, with all the social dislocation this entails. Crime rates are high, and there is a great deal of urban poverty and unemployment. Many children are outside the educational system altogether and standards in state systems, while variable, are generally very low. Environmental problems are especially severe in developing countries.

- Public sector employees in developing countries are generally not well paid, and are more susceptible to corruption than in most developed countries. This lowers their motivation to act in the public interest. So perhaps even more than in developed countries, there is often little relationship between government spending and desirable outcomes. One pointer: an International Monetary Fund (IMF) survey of 50 developing countries concluded that 'there is little empirical evidence to support the claim that public spending improves education and health indicators'.[23]

Despite their smaller administrations, there is no reason why governments in developing countries could not issue Social Policy Bonds and redeem them. They could target broad health, educational and environmental objectives, where improvements could come quite rapidly, and whose achievement could bring large net financial benefits to the government. It is likely that efforts at data collection in most countries would probably have to be strengthened, but that might be easier and more fruitful than enlarging what, in many cases, is a corrupt and incompetent public sector and trusting in that to achieve social objectives.

Unfortunately, even more than in the rich countries, the stated objectives of politicians and governments differ from their real intentions. In many developing countries powerful politicians use their own hidden networks of placemen in key positions in important ministries to frustrate whatever projects or policies they find inconvenient. Outsiders, including especially overseas aid donors, find little correlation between what the governments in these countries say they want and what they do. World Bank and IMF personnel officially judge countries on their stated policies and plans, but in many countries these bear little relationship to the way the country is actually run.[24]

It may be that, in time, aid to these countries could be used to redeem Social Policy Bonds, instead of being given on a government-to-government basis, thereby bypassing corrupt politicians and officials, and the institutions they control. Funds aimed at solving global environmental problems, such as climate change, could similarly reward those who undertook worthwhile projects, rather than corrupt governments. Or corrupt governments could choose to buy globally backed bonds. Their financial self-interest would dictate their modifying their behaviour in favour of targeted global goals. The example of Literacy Bonds illustrates how this might work.

EXAMPLE 2: LITERACY BONDS

Following the attacks on the US on 11 September 2001, a 'war against terrorism' was launched. Probably one of the root causes of terrorism is lack of education. Ignorance lowers people's chance of participating in the global economy. It spawns poverty, cynicism and despair, and entrenches undemocratic and corrupt governments. It creates a fertile ground for the seeds of intolerance and violence.

Assume that as a long-term policy western governments, probably with the help of non-governmental organisations (NGOs) and charities around the world, decide to raise the literacy levels of boys and girls in, say, selected developing countries in the Middle East, North Africa and Asia. This would be an objective that could not be interpreted as cultural imperialism, and that should marginalize extremists, and only extremists. Everybody else would either support it or at least not want to be seen as opposing it. The objective would serve western interests indirectly, by driving a wedge between the terrorists and the poor. But most of all, it would serve the interests of the children in the targeted countries themselves, and so benefit these countries' wider societal interests. It is, in short, a worthwhile end in itself.

The governments of most developing countries already run educational programmes. But there is something half-hearted about many of these governments' commitment to widespread literacy. Sometimes this is literally true, where those in power see education of girls as a threat to the established order. Others place a lower priority on education generally, fearing that it will lead people to question their competence and legitimacy. Or they prefer to spend their countries' limited revenues in less edifying ways—notably on the military.

What is needed then, is a way of increasing literacy that can modify or circumvent governments' uncooperative or obstructive behaviour; a way that can co-opt or subsidise those people in governments who want to help, and at the same time bypass, distract, or otherwise undermine, opposition to the literacy goal. Ideally too, this way would use market forces: the most efficient means yet discovered of allocating society's scarce resources.

'Literacy Bonds' would be a new globally backed, financial instrument, designed to achieve literacy in particular countries. These bonds would be issued on the open market and would become redeemable for a fixed sum *only when literacy reaches an agreed, higher, level.* There would be no need for the people issuing the bonds to make assumptions as to *how* to bring about greater literacy.

Under the Literacy Bond mechanism governments, with the help of NGOs and charities, would collectively decide on the exact specification of their literacy objective, and contribute toward the funds needed to redeem the bonds. As with all Social Policy Bonds, Literacy Bonds would be issued by open tender, as at an auction; those who bid the highest price for the limited number of bonds would be successful in buying them. Each bond would become redeemable for, say, $1 million once the targeted level of literacy, as certified by objective measurements made by independent bodies, had been achieved and sustained. Once issued, the bonds would, of course, be freely tradable.

Literacy Bonds could aim at literacy targets for several countries but assume that bonds are issued that aim to increase 'the number of literate children in Pakistan'. Say Literacy Bonds are issued that would be redeemed only when the literacy in Urdu of Pakistani 7-, 11- and 15-year old girls and boys reached very high levels. Success in achieving this objective could be measured by standardised tests of representative but random samples involving hundreds of Pakistani children. Once issued what would happen? The bonds could be bought by anyone. The Pakistani Government, as the largest current supplier of literacy-increasing services, might decide to buy the bonds, or might be given them, as a form of aid, by the issuers. Either way, it would be in a position to reap financial rewards by doing what it could to increase the literacy of Pakistani schoolchildren. It could do this, not by falsifying the results of literacy tests (which would have to be carried out, or verified by, the bond issuers), but by channelling resources into expanded, increased, or improved, literacy classes. It might, for example, change the school curriculum to give literacy in colloquial Urdu a higher priority, or it could decide to strengthen and enforce laws against truancy. It could broadcast literacy programmes on television and conduct research into the most efficient ways of increasing literacy in its society.

If at any time others thought they could do a better job than the Pakistani Government, they would be in a position to bid more for the Literacy Bonds than their current market value, and buy them from the Government. Similarly if the Government did not want to be actively involved: people and institutions could buy the bonds instead and work to modify or supplement the Pakistani school system's literacy teaching. Bondholders could lobby the Pakistani Government to, say, give a higher priority to literacy in schools, but they could also develop literacy-teaching projects of their own. They might finance literacy classes on TV (originating either in Pakistan or other countries), or set up village schools, or give prizes to the most literate families in villages. It would be up to bondholders to decide on those programmes that would generate the highest increase in literacy per unit outlay. And, as we saw in chapter 4, the market prices of the bonds, and the changes in these prices over time, would supply helpful information as to how fast the objective were being achieved, and whether more funds would be required for this long-term project.

Note that under a Literacy Bond regime, the targeted literacy goal would be more readily achieved by the support and participation of the Pakistani Government, but *it would not rely on such support*. However, it may be that the Pakistani Government would issue bonds itself, with some intellectual (and financial) backing from outsiders. This would be ideal: it would, for instance, streamline necessary legislative changes—the ultimate effect would be to make achievement of the objective quicker and less costly.

The advantages of a Literacy Bond regime over conventional methods of raising literacy would be similar to those arising from other Social Policy Bonds, as described in chapter 4: they include enhanced cost-effectiveness, stability of policy goals for what would most probably be a very long-term objective, and more attractive money flows. And perhaps the further advantage of transparency would have heightened importance with this particular objective. The redemption terms of Literacy Bonds would make clear to everybody exactly what were the objectives of those governments, NGOs, and charities that issued and backed the bonds. It is precisely this transparency of desired outcome that could help build a consensus around the goal of Literacy Bonds. Religious extremists can currently, for example, garner support by saying they oppose mixed schools on moral grounds, but they would be quite isolated if they were openly to oppose the *objective* of more literate schoolgirls. The objective of a Literacy Bond issue would be just that: to increase literacy. It would not so vague or divisive as a 'war on terrorism' with all the excuses such a remit gives for collateral damage and expenditure out of all proportion to positive results. If Literacy Bonds were issued their effect would be to channel the market's incentives and efficiencies into the achievement of one of the international community's most urgent social objectives.

7
Putting it all together

From 'Letters to the Editor', *The Times*, London, 14 August 1999:

> *Yesterday I was told by my doctor that she cannot, at present, refer patients suffering from varicose veins for hospital treatment. Today I read your report that hospital waiting lists have come down. Is this coincidence? Are patients with complaints which, while not life-threatening are extremely irritating and debilitating, being denied treatment so that the Government can maintain that it has fulfilled an election pledge?*

Governments are not used to expressing their objectives in terms of meaningful outcomes, and so are not very good at it. This chapter begins by looking at a few examples of government targets, mostly from the UK, and then discusses criteria for more meaningful policy objectives. It goes on briefly to suggest a range of broad social objectives that would suit a Social Policy Bond regime and look at the limits inherent in quantifiable outcomes and market incentives. Finally it looks at how at a scenario in which Social Policy Bonds assume a dominant role in policymaking.

ENDS AND MEANS

One of the UK Government's current policy objectives is putting 50 per cent of Britain's under-30s into higher education. Like many such targets it sounds worthwhile at first. One might pause for thought though, and ask why 50 per cent? Wouldn't 66 per cent be better? Or 75 per cent? Even the 50 per cent target means, in effect, helping non-academic types go on courses to which they are unsuited and which do very little for their career chances. Neither has past expansion of tertiary education done a great deal to benefit the disadvantaged. It makes employers unnecessarily demanding of job applicants. 'In every developed country, expanding higher education has done less for equal opportunity than one might expect—whilst steering large subsidies towards the middle classes.'[25] Worst of all, perhaps, more funding for higher education means less for literacy and numeracy programmes. There is, of course, nothing wrong with people doing whatever courses they want. But it is highly questionable whether people should be subsidised to do so from a finite educational budget when, for example, about 100 000 children leave school each year in the UK without functional literacy skills[26] and 'eight million people are so poor at reading and writing that they cannot cope with the demands of modern life.'[27]

Often a government's targets show a bias toward more government intervention, when a sector is almost crying out for less of it. So the British farming minister announced in July 2002, an 'action plan', including subsidies, to boost the role of organic farming, and the incoming German Agriculture Minister announced in her maiden speech plans to increase the share of organic farming in German agriculture from 2.5 to 20 per cent over ten years.[28] As with much of the rest of agricultural policy in the rich countries these intentions will almost certainly take the form of significant transfers of resources from the poor who spend more of their income on food, to rich farmers and middle-class consumers. Why not reduce the billions of dollars that subsidise overproduction, and intensifying the pressure on the environment and on food safety? Again, there is nothing actually wrong with organic agriculture, though many of the claims made on its behalf do seem to be overstated.[29] But there is surely something unworthy of a government that wants to micro-manage at public expense what farmers produce and what consumers eat.

Other examples are recycling targets, adopted with enthusiasm, at least at first, by many countries and local authorities. In many cases recycling is helpful to the environment; but there are instances when it probably is not. One life cycle analysis estimated that the manufacture of paper cups consumed 36 times as much electricity and more than 500 times as much wastewater as the manufacture of much-derided polystyrene foam cups.[30] Another study found that while disposable nappies (diapers) create around twice as much trash by volume as recyclable cloth nappies, they are probably more friendly to the environment, consuming less energy than, and half as much water as, cloth nappies. They also generate 40 per cent less air pollution, and 86 per cent less water pollution.[31] Perhaps that's why recycling in many areas has become a sort of pageant, so that concerned households assiduously sort their rubbish into colour-coded bin bags only to find out later that all the bags were thrown onto the same landfill once they were safely out of view.[32]

More higher education, organic agriculture and recycling…what is the root cause of the problem? Essentially this: policymakers see more university students, more organic farming, and more recycling as *ends in themselves* rather than means to ends, and the results have been unfortunate, to put it mildly. There *are* environmental problems that could be solved by recycling, or organic farming, just as there are certain social and environmental problems that certain, highly specific forms of higher education might solve. But vague, unfocussed programmes, applied uniformly across entire economies, do little to help.

This sort of policymaking has already had far-reaching effects on society. Perverse subsidies of the kind described in chapter 1, subsidies to certain forms of infrastructure and an overly prescriptive regulatory environment are inherently biased against smaller, local producers, and in favour of larger businesses with global reach.[33]

A Social Policy Bond regime would not allow policymakers to get away with targets that have disguised or meaningless goals. Its targets would actually be society's objectives, or at least they would be very closely correlated with society's objectives. When bonds were issued, people would not be told *how* to achieve a targeted objective. So the ways in which they would try to achieve it could not be assumed. This would force a clarity missing from today's policymaking, whereby government ministers can announce policies that *imply*, but do not necessarily reward, outcomes. So a blandly appealing policy target, like increasing the share of organic agriculture, can represent in people's minds a cleaner environment and improved food safety. But if government were clear about its goals and were genuinely prepared to help bring about a cleaner environment and improved food safety it would *set explicit targets for environmental and food safety outcomes*, and give people the chance to work out the best ways of achieving them.

Many current targets may also be too narrow. One UK local authority is targeting drug abuse amongst youths.[34] This may, however, be less efficient than targeting youth deaths or sickness generally, whether by issuing Social Policy Bonds or not. If drug abuse amongst youths is targeted, that might mean people give a lower priority to, say, road accident deaths or injuries, and that in turn might be less efficient than targeting deaths, sickness and injuries amongst youths generally. In fact, it is arguable that reduced infant mortality and other health indicators like longevity of the whole population should be subsumed into a single health objective. People could then allocate life-extending resources to maximise their impact on all members of society's life expectancy (perhaps adjusted by a quality-of-life factor). In efficiency terms alone, that is, in terms of extra person-years of (quality-adjusted) life saved per unit outlay, it would probably be more efficient to target that broader indicator. Chapter 2 looked at the possibility that if Social Policy Bonds were to target one pollutant, there could be a consequent increase in emissions of other, untargeted, pollutants. When deciding how broad a targeted objective should be, much would depend on how self-contained were complementary targets: that is, on how readily resources would flow away from achieving some societal goals when another goal were targeted. That would depend partly on how the objective would interact with institutional structures and funding. An objective that could realistically be achieved very quickly might be less likely to bring about a significant reordering of priorities; but a narrow, longer term objective could lead to inefficient shifts of resources away from non-targeted objectives. In general though, and to reiterate the point made in chapter 2: objectives that are complementary and that, if not pursued jointly, could conflict, should be targeted by a single bond issue.

Why not then target a single 'quality of life' indicator for the whole of society, taking into account all quantifiable social and environmental objectives: quality of life, longevity, education level, environmental pollution, crime, homelessness unemployment, leisure time and any others? Surely targeting one single aggregated 'social welfare' indicator would be the optimal approach?

There are two reasons why attempting this would be inadvisable. The first is the daunting practical problem of defining a meaningful and measurable indicator of social welfare. The second is even more fundamental. Aiming for an increase in a single social welfare indicator carries with it an assumption that society's needs can be traded off against each other. But for many of the needs for which government usually assumes responsibility such trade-offs cannot be made. For the neediest beneficiaries of government's welfare programmes, a massive increase in priority for, say, health care would be unlikely to compensate for a total withdrawal of government funds from, say, basic education. 'Safety net' programmes, by definition, are scarcely amenable to trade-offs. In the same way a lowering of the crime rate, however welcome, could hardly compensate for the total collapse of a country's physical environment.

OBJECTIVES FOR A BOND REGIME

So what should society choose to target? The choice of outcomes for targeting by a bond regime would obviously be a matter for discussion, negotiation and constant refinement. The transparency inherent in the targeting of desired outcomes would help these processes. What follows are some suggestions arising from the author's view of where government's comparative advantage lies; they fall into two categories.

1 Helping the poor and disadvantaged

Tackling poverty and the consequences of poverty is a large part of government's declared rationale for supplying health, education, housing, and welfare services as well as most of its transfer payments. It also implicitly underpins much government intervention in infrastructure, industry and agriculture; though 'strategic' arguments are often also deployed in those contexts.

The rationale for using government-issued Social Policy Bonds to eradicate poverty is that the poor are most in need of government intervention, and also because it is at lower levels of real income that the correlation between a quantifiable indicator and social welfare is strong and therefore useful to policymakers.[35] A bond regime targeting broad indicators such as longevity, or basic educational achievement, would divert resources to where they could do most good: that is, where the maximum benefit per dollar outlay could be achieved, and it is those who are most disadvantaged who would benefit from channelling of funds in this way. A bond regime would focus government interventions more successfully than the current system. Its explicit objectives would be aimed at helping the poorest and most disadvantaged members of society. It could not get sidetracked, or corrupted, into supporting the better off or big business *at the expense* of the poor.

Suggested objectives aimed at helping the poor and disadvantaged are:

- Improved basic education and training

- Lower unemployment

- Better physical health

- Better mental health

- Reduced homelessness.

2 Public goods

The rationale for the government supplying these goods is that they cannot be supplied by the private sector with any efficiency. Suggested categories for goals would be:

- Law and order

- National defence

- Environmental goods.

LIMITATIONS

Anything that exists, exists in some quantity, and can therefore be measured. Lord Kelvin[36]

Social Policy Bonds would target quantifiable outcomes. In traditional societies, where people lived closer to each other, people probably knew a lot more about each other's general state of happiness. They knew when the people that mattered most to them were happy, and they had a fairly good idea of what would make them happy. In our industrial societies, with their large, complex economies, government bodies have largely taken over from extended families and local people in supplying a range of welfare services, or the cash to pay for them. Increasingly government is using numerical indicators to formulate policy.

But this use of indicators is relatively recent, unsystematic and unsophisticated. Few indicators are targeted explicitly for a sustained period: the targeted range of inflation is a rare (and not especially helpful) exception, as is the coherent range of indicators presented in the UK Government's attempt to tackle poverty.[37] More commonly targeted indicators, such as the size of hospital waiting lists, don't measure what matters to people or are prone to manipulation. Even when goals are clear and meaningful they are rarely costed, and they are almost always too narrow. Those broad targets that are targeted with some degree of consistency tend to be economic aggregates, such as the inflation rate, or the rate of growth of Gross Domestic Product—which appears to be *de facto* indicator par excellence of rich and poor countries alike. But GDP's shortcomings as a single indicator of the health of an economy are well known: amongst other failings, GDP does not take into account changes in the quality of the environment, or the distribution of income, it ignores human capital (the education and skills that are embodied in the work force) and leisure time, and it ignores such social problems as crime and homelessness. Under a bond regime statistics like GDP would never assume the authority they appear to have nowadays.[38] The goals of government policy would be meaningful social and environmental outcomes, not growth rates or other economic indicators.

But, just as under the current regime, desired outcomes would have to be represented by numerical indicators. It would appear that the choice will increasingly be between (a) the current de facto targeting of GDP along with an almost random array of narrow, easily manipulated indicators that have no necessary relationship to societal goals, and (b) the targeting of consistent, transparent, mutually supportive indicators that represent meaningful social outcomes.

Obviously this author would prefer the latter, but it should be recognised that even that when following that approach policymakers would need to be guided by the limitations inherent in quantifiable indicators. The policy implication would be that *government should limit its role to those areas where numbers are helpful.* It is generally at low levels of health, educational level, housing, income, caloric intake etc, that increases are strongly correlated with an individual's welfare. But beyond basic levels, individuals' ultimate objectives are for the most part inescapably subjective. They cannot be measured, nor can the societal counterpart of social welfare, and government should recognise this limitation. It can never know as much about people's happiness as other people. Lord Kelvin's remark is, of course, false. An individual's happiness, or its aggregate counterpart for society as a whole, *cannot* be summed up by any conceivable array of quantifiable measures. Some things simply cannot be measured, and the government would do well not to get involved with them.

If numerical indicators are limited, so too is self-interest as a motivating force. People perform valuable social or environmental services not only for monetary gain, but also because they enjoy doing them for their own sake, or because they believe them to be the morally right things to do, or because they believe that their actions will advance some cause to which they are committed. These 'intrinsic' motives are different from external, monetary incentives. Offering monetary rewards might 'crowd out' these less mercenary and more civic-minded motivations or even undermine them. Bruno Frey, a Swiss economist, has researched and written about this effect.[39] Crowding out internal motivation can occur, he writes, because, monetary incentives can undermine people's feelings of self-determination and self-esteem. Also, when external incentives are supplied, the 'person acting on the basis of his or her intrinsic motivation is deprived of the chance to exhibit this intrinsic motivation to other persons.' Not mentioned by Frey, but also plausible is that financial incentives can undermine the cognitive outlook that sees socially and environmentally beneficial services as worthwhile in their own right, rather than as a cost for which compensation and payments must be paid by taxpayers.[40]

While these considerations would have implications for a bond regime, they apply to some degree to existing policy methods. But as

Frey says, crowding-out effects are not always significant. In markets, based on relations amongst essentially self-interested strangers, financial incentives as exhibited through the price effect do work as classical economics predicts. That is, they work to increase supply. And when (as they would be under a bond regime) external rewards are seen as recognition of the importance of, say, civic duty rather than an attempt to 'buy' one's civic performance, they may well support, rather than undermine, moral and other intrinsic motivations.[41] A bond regime could give bondholders incentives to further Frey's research, exploring the relationships between financial incentives and supply of civic performance. They could use this knowledge to minimise the costs of achieving targeted objectives by, for example, finding out when monetary incentives are least likely to supplant the intrinsic motivations of people who help achieve objectives, and concentrating their use in those circumstances.

THE FUTURE

Government focused on outcomes would blur the distinction between the public and policymakers. People would take more of an interest in politics encouraged by the direct link between policy and outcomes. There would be less ambiguity, and less ideology. No longer would politicians be able to claim that simply by increasing expenditure in, say, health, they were addressing society's health care concerns.

People would have higher expectations of what their taxes can achieve. They would be more aware that extra expenditure on, for example, keeping street crime down, might mean a worsening of local air quality. Single-issue campaigners might find themselves engaging more realistically with political realities.

Intra-country comparisons, already compiled in many countries, would take on new significance. People in one city or region seeing, for example, that the level of basic educational achievement of their children was lower than in other cities, might vote for more of their local taxes to reduce that disparity. They would not be discouraged by the fact that they were not educational experts; nor would they look to central government or educational professionals for the answer. Their focus would be on the priority they give to the educational goal as against other social goals.

At the national level, the most obscene wastes of taxpayers' money would disappear. Transfers and subsidies would be delivered to those who evidently need it. People would be given income support because they satisfied some objective criteria saying they were poor; not because they had deceived the public or played on its emotions. Industrialists and farmers who benefit from the wide array of disguised and perverse subsidies, transfers, and import barriers, would lose out, at least in the short term. Instead funds would be devoted to redeeming Social Policy Bonds that generate employment and other social benefits at least cost.

Eventually a wide range of social and environmental priorities would be achieved through Social Policy Bonds though others, such as defence, would probably continue to be supplied by government employees for many decades.

A coherent, explicit range of meaningful social and environmental goals is but one of the two essential elements underpinning the Social Policy Bond concept. The other is market forces. The combination of two elements should generate better social outcomes more cost-effectively. Governments or people would have more money to spend or more leisure time, or both, which could benefit society in many ways.

Resources are always going to be limited and Social Policy Bonds would not change that. Priorities and choices will always have to be made: under the Social Policy Bond principle, governments would still decide on which problems to solve, and on the sums allocated to their solution. But democratic governments are good at representing and articulating their people's wishes. Where they are not so successful is in working out the most efficient ways of achieving these goals. This achievement is really a matter of allocating scarce resources. In economic theory, and on all the evidence, markets are the best way of allocating scarce resources to achieve prescribed ends. Social Policy Bonds would allow both government and the market to do what each is best at doing: respectively: prescribing ends, and allocating resources to meet these ends.

In the long run the widespread acceptance that self-interest can be channelled into solving social problems could have more far-reaching implications. International transfers of taxpayer funds appear to be at least as prone to misallocation as their domestic equivalents. International or global social or environmental problems such as malnutrition or climate change could be made the targets of future Social Policy Bonds. Corrupt governments could be major purchasers of such bonds. Or they could be paid by major bondholders to alter their policies. Either way, they would have incentives to modify their behaviour to help achieve these desired outcomes, whether these include ensuring that food supplies reach their own starving citizens, or doing what they can to achieve trans-boundary objectives such as global environmental goals. Social Policy Bonds would be more likely to be effective than current aid programmes, because bondholders could benefit only by actually solving targeted social and environmental problems.

Internationally backed Social Policy Bonds targeting poverty, malnutrition or deadly conflicts are most probably a long way into the future. Before then, Social Policy Bonds would probably have to be issued on a smaller scale, gradually refined, and become widely and successfully deployed at the national level.

For government to relinquish most of its discretion as to how to achieve social and environmental goals would require some courage as well as humility. Yet in doing so, a government would not be renouncing its existing sanctions against illegal acts. It would still be defining society's goals, and it would still be the ultimate source of finance for achieving them. In fact, the current system, when viewed impartially, would appear to be far more irrational. Under it, large proportions of national income are spent in pursuit of nebulous goals, few of which are costed, many of which conflict with each other, and many of which primarily benefit the better off—some of them already very wealthy indeed. Administering this expenditure is a burgeoning bureaucracy, which, on the rare occasions its performance is even measured, is almost invariably shown to be woefully inefficient. With a massive public sector, and after decades of ever-increasing taxation, the British Government today is still targeting the birth weight of babies in the country's most disadvantaged areas.[42]

The acceptance of a Social Policy Bond regime, even with the aim of achieving national goals as uncontroversial as lower crime rates, or better health and education outcomes, may be politically difficult, and must be a gradual process. But the potential benefits should not be ignored. By injecting market forces into the achievement of social and environmental goals, Social Policy Bonds could achieve these goals more cost-effectively.

Epilogue

The Social Policy Bond idea has had an unusual fate for an unusual idea. It has been in the public domain for about 14 years, and it has not been so far been adopted anywhere, to my knowledge. But neither has it been dismissed outright. It tends to provoke initial enthusiasm amongst economists and decision makers, but then to be forgotten as other more pressing issues arise. Robert Shiller, Professor of Economics at Yale University, wrote to me at the end of 1996, praising the Social Policy Bond idea, saying that it creates "a large interest group for the solution of important problems. The political and other effects of creating such an interest group could be incalculable." An earlier draft of this book elicited extreme comments at both ends of the range from the two referees: one dismissed the text as an irrelevance. The other called the idea "original and ingenious" and "a substantial contribution to debate about public policy".

In April 2002, I presented a paper on the bond concept to joint meeting of the Agriculture and Environment Committees at the Organisation for Economic Cooperation and Development (OECD) in Paris. At the meeting, delegations from most of the OECD's member countries made comments on the paper. These were mostly along the lines of "this is very interesting—but unworkable in practice." But one of the delegates perhaps articulated the deeper feelings of those present, who were overwhelmingly government employees: "if this gets adopted we'll all be out of jobs!"

I am pleased though that, at the time of writing, certain private individuals have taken the initiative and are proposing to issue their own Social Policy Bonds. They are considering floating bonds for projects as diverse as boosting voter registration, raising literacy in developing countries and developing open-source software. Enthused by the bond concept, they are raising funds, or preparing to put up their own funds, to redeem bonds targeting objectives that they specify. I am heartened and encouraged by their efforts.

Bibliography

Investing for the future, Ronnie Horesh, UK CEED Bulletin No 35, Centre for Economic and Environmental Development, Cambridge, UK, September-October 1991. (Presented as Room Document 3 to the December 1994 meeting of the OECD Joint Working Party of the Committee for Agriculture and the Environment Policy Committee.)

Social Policy Bonds: Injecting market incentives into the solution of social problems), Ronnie Horesh, AEU Occasional Papers, University of Cambridge, Cambridge, UK, August 1992.

Injecting incentives into the solution of social problems: Social Policy Bonds, Ronnie Horesh, Economic Affairs, **20** (3), Institute of Economic Affairs, London, September 2000.

Injecting incentives into the solution of social and environmental problems: Social Policy Bonds, Ronnie Horesh, iUniversity Press, Lincoln, Nebraska, USA. ISBN: 0-595-15374-7, January 2001.

Better than Kyoto: how Climate Stability Bonds can inject market incentives into the achievement of a stable climate, Ronnie Horesh, Writers Club Press, USA. ISBN: 0-595-21164-X, December 2001.

Better than Kyoto: Climate Stability Bonds, Ronnie Horesh, Economic Affairs, **22** (3), Institute of Economic Affairs, London, September 2002.

Websites

http://www.geocities.com/socialpbonds *Social Policy Bonds*: the first three papers listed under 'Bibliography' can be downloaded free of charge from this site, which also contains links to online retailers of the book cited as the remaining bibliographic reference, and the email address of the author of this book.

http://users.rcn.com/wware1/spb-game.html *SPB the game*: online simulation of Social Policy Bonds.

http://www.openknowledge.org/writing/open-source/scb/ *The Wall Street Performer Protocol*. Using Software Completion Bonds to fund open source software development.

Endnotes

[1]. Paul Atkinson and Paul van den Noord, *Managing public expenditure: some emerging policy issues and a framework for analysis,* Economics Department Working Papers no. 285, OECD, 2001.

[2]. *Agricultural policies in OECD countries: monitoring and evaluation 2002,* OECD, Paris, 2002.

[3]. *Distributional effects of agricultural support in selected OECD countries,* OECD, Paris, 1999.

[4]. P Waugh, *British watchdog criticises EU as fraud soars 75% to 700m,* The Independent, 30 May 2002.

[5]. These figures come from *Perverse Incentives: Subsidies and Sustainable Development,* A P G de Moor, Institute for Research on Public Expenditure, The Netherlands, 1996: **http:// www.worldpolicy.organisation/Americas/environment/ subsidies.html.**

[6]. Julian Le Grand, *The strategy of equality: redistribution and the social services,* George Allen and Unwin, London, 1982. The author points out that a major declared objective of government spending on social services has always been redistribution of wealth to the poor. But, after examining the impact of public expenditure on health, education, housing and transport in the UK, he concluded that in almost all the forms he scrutinised, it was distributed in favour of the higher social groups. Although

the details of his results are obviously not up-to-date, the general features are still relevant.

[7]. ibid

[8]. Ross Clark, *The great granny grab*, The Spectator, London, 17 August 2002.

[9]. *Country File*, BBC1 television, UK, 8 February 1998.

[10]. See Hayek, F A, 'The Pretence of Knowledge', in his *New Studies in Philosophy, Politics, Economics and the History of Ideas*, University of Chicago Press, Chicago, 1978.

[11]. Excerpts are from Article 39.

[12]. See, for example, *Happiness is a warm vote*, The Economist, 17 April 1999.

[13]. See *Alternative endings*, Radio Times, 13 July 2002. This was the subject of a Channel 4 documentary *Death: you're better off with cancer*, broadcast on 16 July 2002.

[14]. See bibliography for details of this author's book on Climate Stability Bonds.

[15]. See, for example, the references cited by J T Overpeck, in *Climate Change: The Hole Record*, Nature **403**, 714-715, 17 February 2000.

[16]. *The Great Promise of the 'Greenhouse Effect*, Sylvan H Wittwer, Consumers Research, June 1997.

[17]. *The Balance Sheet*, John Kay, *Prospect*, July 2002.

[18]. John Kay, op cit.

[19]. Dr Jonathan Michie, Lecturer at the Judge Institute of Management Studies, and a Fellow of Robinson College, Cambridge, UK, speaking at a seminar on *The Elusive Concept of Sovereignty*, held at the Finnish Institute in April 1996.

[20]. Allen Schick, *The spirit of reform: managing the New Zealand state sector in a time of change*, State Services Commission, Wellington, 1996.

[21]. Arthur Andersen and Enterprise LSE, *Value for money drivers in the Private Finance Initiative,* commissioned by (UK) Treasury Taskforce, 17 January 2000.

[22]. Arthur Andersen and Enterprise LSE, op cit.

[23]. Anjeev Gupta, Marijn Verhoeven and Erwin Tiongson, *Does higher government spending buy better results in education and health care?*, IMF Working Paper WP/99/21, February 1999.

[24]. *Africa: the heart of the matter*, The Economist, 13 May 2000.

[25]. Alison Wolf, *Too many students*, Prospect, July 2002.

[26]. BBC News Online, 2 December, 1999.

[27]. International Adult Literacy Survey, 1998, (figure of eight million applies to Britain). This Survey also says that while in Britain over 20% of the population falls into the low skills category; in Europe the figure is around 10%.

[28]. Bettina Wassener, *Green minister pushes for farming reform: One in five farms will be organic in 10 years' time if the government's policy goes according to plan,* Financial Times London, 12 June 2001.

[29]. See, for instance, Anthony Trewavas, *Urban myths of organic farming*, Nature **410,** 22 March 2001.

[30]. Martin B Hocking, *Paper versus polystyrene: a complex choice,* Science **251**, pp 504-5, 1 February 1991.

[31]. Franklin Associates, *Energy and environmental profile analysis of children's disposable and cloth diapers*, Franklin Associates Ltd, Prairie Village, KS, USA, July 1990.

[32]. For example, in Chester, UK: see Chester Standard, June 2002, and *Waste of time,* The Economist, 6 July 2002 (page 48), about recycling in New York.

[33]. Steven Gorelick (principal author): *Small is beautiful, big is subsidised,* International Society for Ecology and Culture, Dartington, England 1998.

[34]. *Target 2000,* Cheshire County Council, 1999.

[35]. See *Happiness is a warm vote,* The Economist, 17 April 1999.

[36]. quoted by John Adams, in *Risk,* University College London Press, 1995.

[37]. Department of Social Security, Poverty and Social Exclusion Team, *Opportunity for All—Tackling Poverty and Social Exclusion,* 1-11 John Adam Street, London WC2N 6HT, September 1999.

[38]. See E J Mishan, *The costs of economic growth,* Staples Press, 1967, for a discussion of 'index economics'.

[39]. Bruno S Frey, *Not just for the money: an economic theory of personal motivation,* Edward Elgar, 1997.

[40]. Gerald F Gaus, *Crowding out virtue,* Agenda, **5** (4), Australian National University, 1998. This is a short review of Bruno Frey's book, cited above.

[41]. Gaus, op cit.

[42]. Department of Social Security, op cit.

0-595-24823-3

www.ingramcontent.com/pod-product-compliance
Lightning Source LLC
Chambersburg PA
CBHW030840180526
45163CB00004B/1393